Money Road Trip

Chart your Course to Financial Freedom

🌐 linktr.ee/drbrendau

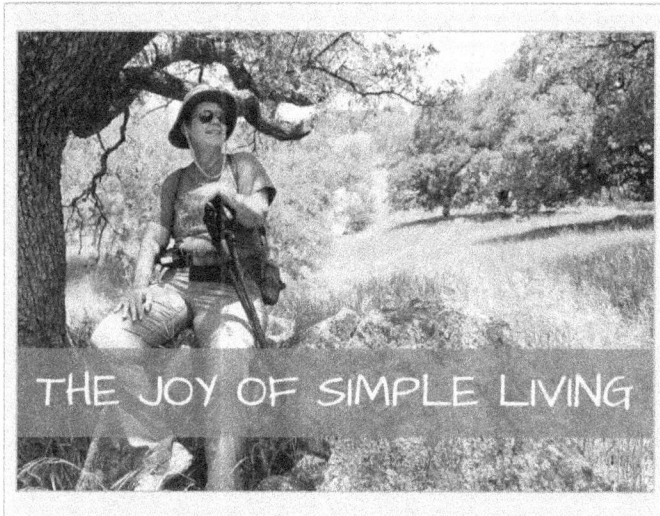

THE JOY OF SIMPLE LIVING

Check out Dr. Brenda's RV lifestyle in this mini-documentary.

bit.ly/drbrendaumovie

Published by B.K. Uekert Enterprises, LLC
5753 Hwy 85 N #2660
Crestview, FL 32536

ISBN 979-8-9895861-0-3

For London

you can do it

Roadmap

Your Road Trip

In May 2020, I took a leap of faith, swapping my house keys for an RV, and set off on an adventure that promised to be a life-changer. And indeed, it's been an extraordinary journey. I've traveled across the nation's vast landscapes, immersed myself in the untamed beauty of secluded trails, witnessed breathtaking sunsets, and forged friendships with fellow nomads. Each mile traversed has been a chapter in itself, filled with stories and discoveries.

Writing a book on financial freedom, I couldn't think of a better metaphor than a road trip. Why? Because managing finances should be an exhilarating journey, not a mundane task. Money, after all, is the ticket to unlocking dreams and seizing opportunities. Sure, the road might have its share of bumps, sudden stops, and unexpected detours. But the destination? It's nothing short of extraordinary. It's a place where you're the architect of your life, charting a course towards a future filled with possibility.

This road trip has taught me that everyone has their unique travel style. There are the boondockers who find solace in the wilderness; the national park enthusiasts who seek adventure right outside their door; and the luxury-seekers who prefer their journeys with a touch of comfort. This diversity in travel styles mirrors the journey to financial freedom. There is no one right way; understanding your personal preferences is crucial to discovering your path.

This book took shape in my RV, with the final manuscript completed in the solitude of Death Valley National Park. While I am at the wheel, guiding you through this journey, I owe a great deal to my digital companion, ChatGPT. This AI companion was my steadfast editor, a whiz at smoothing out the tone, sprinkling in just the right adjectives, and breathing life into my anecdotes.

As you embark on your own journey toward financial freedom, remember to enjoy the ride. Stop at those hidden gems along the way. Absorb the beauty of the landscapes. This journey is more than reaching a destination; it's a celebration of life's experiences, a feast for the senses. Embrace every new discovery, every challenge, and every moment of joy. Enjoy the ride!

1

LOGISTICS

Road Trip!!

Nothing beats a good road trip! Imagine a beautiful sunny day driving on the open road, just you and your besties singing along to your favorite tunes. There's the anticipation of reaching an amazing destination where the party can begin. Oh, but the trip itself is filled with stories, laughter, and lightheartedness. It's a time to leave your worries behind, if only for a little while.

Road Map

- a detailed plan to guide progress toward a goal

A great road trip doesn't just happen. You've got to check schedules, agree on the destination, and find the money to have a super time - all before you can even think about hopping in the car. You need a road map to guide you. Consider this workbook your road map to financial freedom.

Sometimes, the journey is even more memorable than the destination. And like the best road trips, I want you to have FUN along the way. So I designed this Workbook as an interactive piece of art. Here's your first hazard warning!

HAZARD: Be Bold. Be true to yourself as you navigate this Workbook. This is the time to admit your failings, explore the limitations you've placed on yourself, and make a strong and loud commitment to create a better life. Don't hold back and don't judge. Be YOU!

This Book is Organized for Success

The world of personal finance is often a snooze. It's dense material slammed with mind-numbing jargon and complicated theories. That's NOT this workbook. Here we keep it basic and simple, and we have FUN on the road.

We have nine stops on our road trip to financial freedom. Each stop starts off with clear instructions - you'll receive a Big Mission, Objectives, and a To-Do Checklist. This Workbook is designed to help you achieve one big goal: Build your your personal roadmap to financial freedom.

Road Trip Icons

Every road trip has its ups and downs and times when the GPS fails. You'll find icons scattered throughout our road trip. Here's what's ahead of you.

HAZARD: Reminders and tips to be true to yourself and to check your mindset at the curb.

FUEL STOP: Motivational and inspirational quotes that will fuel your trip.

Make a Mess!

This is your time to play. Here are some tips for completing this Workbook:

- Grab some pens, colored pencils, markers, sticky notes, glitter - hey, whatever rocks your boat.
- Devote some quiet time to spend alone with your Workbook. It's better to spend 15 minutes of focused time than 2 hours mixed with distractions.
- Get your head in a good place. Play some of your favorite music in the background.
- Make a mess of this Workbook! Scribble. Highlight. Add stickers. Make it meaningful.
- Remember: No Judging! This is your story - and it's your path to an awesome future. Don't knock yourself for past mistakes.

For more tools to fuel your financial journey, swing by the Money Road Trip website. There, you'll discover an array of helpful resources like custom spreadsheets, comprehensive toolkits, and an engaging online course – all designed to be your trusty companions as you cruise towards financial freedom.

MRT
MoneyRoadTrip.com

moneyroadtrip.com

Ready . . . Set . . . Start!

Congratulations on being here! Let's get the show on the road. Commit! Write down your goal here.

SMARTER =
- Specific
- Measurable
- Actionable
- Relevant
- Time-bound
- Evaluate
- Reward

_____'s   Goal
(your name)

I will complete this workbook by   _____
(date)

I will accomplish this by . . .

(Examples: devoting 30 minutes every day to my workbook; completing a new chapter every week, etc.)

[ ]

I will evaluate my progress and refine my goal on a (weekly/bi-weekly) basis.
(circle one)

When I complete this workbook, I will reward myself by . . .

(Your goal is financial freedom, so keep your rewards sensible! Examples: hosting game night, a new book, your favorite pizza, a mini-road trip to a local destination).

[ ]

Thoughts & Notes

Notes

2

DESTINATION: FREEDOM

Destination: Freedom

Welcome to the first stop on your epic Money Road Trip! In this chapter, we're setting our sights on our destination – Financial Freedom. This is where the magic begins, where your dreams start to take shape, and where you'll discover what financial freedom truly means to you.

Objectives

- To discover the meaning of financial freedom

- To identify your values and priorities

Big Mission

Our mission is to uncover your unique definition of financial freedom and lay the foundation for an inspiring journey toward it.

To-do Checklist

- [ ] Write about your dream life

- [ ] List your values and priorities

- [ ] Complete this: Financial Freedom means . . .

- [ ] Get excited about your future!!

Discover the Meaning of Financial Freedom

So here we are together, traveling toward this magical place we call "financial freedom." Later on, we'll put some price tags on our destination, but today, it's all about dreaming. On this road trip, we're all about building a life without money worries. But it's about so much more than that.

Financial Freedom

The state of having control and flexibility over your financial life. It means that you have the financial resources and stability to make choices that align with your values and desires, without being constrained by money-related concerns.

Financial freedom means something different for each person. Below are four features of financial freedom. <u>Rank each item by writing a number in the star. Use 1 for the most important and 4 for the least important.</u>

Freedom from Financial Stress: You no longer worry about covering your basic needs, managing debt, or handling unexpected expenses. Financial freedom brings peace of mind.

Pursuing Your Passions: You can chase your dreams, explore your passions, and engage in activities that bring you joy, whether they are related to work, travel, hobbies, or charitable endeavors.

Generosity and Impact: Financial freedom enables you to give back to your community or support causes you're passionate about, creating a positive impact on the world.

Time Freedom: You have more options to use your time as you see fit, whether that means more time with family, pursuing hobbies, or enjoying leisure activities.

Financial freedom has a personal and deep meaning for each of us. It's about so much more than just having a specific amount of money in the bank; it's about crafting a life that aligns with your values, passions, and aspirations. It's about reaching a point where you have the freedom to make choices that make your heart sing, without constantly worrying about money.

As you embark on this adventure, remember that your financial freedom journey is uniquely yours. It's not about keeping up with the Joneses or conforming to societal expectations. It's about defining your own path and creating a future that reflects your deepest desires. Let's hit the road and discover what financial freedom truly means to you!

Kate's Beach Life

Kate dreamed about waking up in a cozy beachfront cottage with the sound of seagulls in the distance. She could almost smell the aroma of freshly brewed coffee as she stepped onto her private veranda, overlooking the azure waters. Those dreams kept her going through long Midwestern winters and stressful days at the office. She knew the formula for financial freedom - grow your income, lower your expenses, and save and invest the difference. And she knew that she could turn her dreams into a reality.

And then came the day when Kate reached the point where she felt comfortable leaving her corporate job and leaping into a lifestyle that fed her soul. She downsized her home and used the proceeds to fund her travel adventures. Kate's mornings often start with sunrise yoga on the beach, followed by exploring new cultures and cuisines. Her career as a freelance writer allows her the flexibility to work from anywhere, making her dream life a reality.

For Kate, those idyllic beach days were just a part of the dream. It was about building a flexible work schedule, and pursuing her passions. Put yourself in Kate's sandals. Now you might not be a beach enthusiast, but picture yourself engaged in work that you're deeply passionate about, whether it's writing, painting, or running your own business from the comfort of your home. You have the freedom to choose your projects and work on things that ignite your creativity and bring fulfillment. Now isn't that worth pursuing!

Your Dream Life

What's your dream life? I'll bet it's been forever since you thought about how you could shape your life . . . if only you had more money, and more time. Hey, this is our road trip, and I'm granting you your wish. In our little world, money and time aren't constraints. Imagine, that you just won ONE YEAR of Freedom - the freedom to do whatever you want. The freedom to be without bills or debt or money worries. The freedom to leave your job behind for an entire year. And maybe, just maybe, you can find a way to extend that year into two years, five years, ten years, even a lifetime? How does that life look to you?

△ **HAZARD: You gotta believe! Watch out for these 3 potholes**

Dreaming requires us to step back from the realities of life. We have to get out of our own way. So before we begin this activity, let go of these limitations and open your life to a world of possibilities. Check each hazard that applies to you.

☐ **MINDSET** - there's just no way I can really make my dreams happen. I don't have the courage. And if I try, I know I'll fail. Nothing ever changes - I can't do this!

☐ **REALITY**- I'm just trying to survive, day-to-day. I'm too busy for this foolishness. Besides, given my current situation, I can never reach my dreams.

☐ **EXPECTATIONS** - People have certain expectations of me. What will they think if I suddenly start chasing my dreams? I have expectations and obligations to meet.

in this moment, I want you to speed right over those potholes. Here's your road trip mantra!

I WILL make my dreams happen.

Reality is about today. I have the power to shape tomorrow. I will create a NEW reality.

I am a unique and wonderful person. I deserve a dream life that fills me with joy and meaning.

This is YOUR road trip. Your journey will be like no one else's. Believe in yourself! There may be times when self-doubt enters your travels. Always remember: You are strong, courageous, and worthy.

Let's dive deep into your imagination and create a rich, detailed picture of your dream life. Find a quiet and comfortable space where you can fully immerse yourself in this exercise. Here's a step-by-step guide to help you visualize your financial freedom dream:

Set the Scene

Begin by closing your eyes and taking a few deep, calming breaths. Imagine yourself in a place that brings a smile to your face. It's a place that makes your heart sing. Maybe you know the exact location. Or maybe you have a general sense of where you'd like to be in your dream life? Think about where you are - mountains, city, country, beach, desert, forests, etc. Set the scene for us. Be as detailed as you can. Remember, put those doubts aside. This is your dream time!

Here's a favorite scene from my dream life. (Describe the setting and how it makes you feel.)

Build your Home

Now let's talk about your home. Is it a comfortable single family house in the suburbs, a cottage on the beach, a condo in the best part of town, a nice cabin in the woods, or a glitzy mansion with amazing views? Or maybe you seek the nomadic life - RVing or sailing around the world? Picture every detail, from the color of its exterior to the atmosphere inside. Take us on walk of your lovely home.

Figure out Work

Wow! You're doing a great job. Let's keep going!

How does work fit into your dream life? Are you working . . . or are your days carefree? Here are some options. Shade the button that best represents the way you see work fitting into your dream life.

○ I'd like to be working full-time - either at my current position or one similar to it.

○ I'll probably be working full-time, but I may switch careers or become an entrepreneur. I'd like to do something that I feel more passionate about.

○ I think I'd like to work part-time, or maybe free-lance and decide my own schedule. I'd like to keep a steady income, but free up more time for myself.

○ I don't want to work at a job. I might "work" as a volunteer and donate my services. But my dream life doesn't include a regular job or career.

○ I have a different idea altogether. (write it below)

"The biggest adventure you can take is to live the life of your dreams."
— Oprah Winfrey

Capture Your Perfect Day

Are you ready for the fun part? Visualize a day in your dream life. What does it look like? Where are you? Who are you with? Imagine the details of your surroundings, activities, and emotions. Use the space below to write all about your day.

Now how do you feel about the vision you just created? Are you secretly smiling as you think about how you want to live - oh, if only you could fly in a rocket to the land of financial freedom!

A World of Possibilities with Diego and Riley

The Vision

Diego and Riley shared a vision of a life filled with adventure, connection, and meaningful work. They imagined a world where they could escape the daily grind, explore new horizons, and spend quality time with their children. Their dream life was a blend of travel, entrepreneurship, and intentional living.

In their vision, they saw themselves living in a charming duplex in a vibrant town, surrounded by a lively community and exciting opportunities. Mornings would start with strolls through the bustling streets and family breakfasts in their cozy duplex. They dreamed of having the freedom to work on projects they were passionate about while being fully present for their children's milestones. Travel remained a central part of their vision, with regular family adventures to exotic destinations, immersing themselves in new cultures and experiences.

The Journey

To turn their dream into reality, Diego and Riley purchased a duplex in town. They recognized the income potential it offered, allowing them to generate revenue that funded their dream life. They became landlords, and their duplex became a source of financial stability.

Diego and Riley also transitioned to remote work arrangements, which provided them with the flexibility to maintain their careers while having the freedom to travel with their children. Their entrepreneurship endeavors, including a family-focused blog and YouTube channel, continued to flourish, connecting them with a like-minded community of adventurers.

The Dream

Today, Diego and Riley are living their dream life in their lively town. They wake up to the energy of the community, spending mornings exploring the local markets, and cherishing family moments in their stylish duplex. Their remote work allows them to balance career commitments with the joys of parenting, providing them with the freedom to be there for their children.

Their family adventures have taken them to destinations within their own country and across the globe, enriching their lives with diverse cultures and unforgettable experiences. Their duplex, serving as both a home and a source of income, has become a cornerstone of their financial freedom journey.

Diego and Riley's story continues to serve as a testament to the power of determination, creativity, and strategic financial planning. Their vision of a life filled with adventure, connection, and meaningful work has evolved into a vibrant reality, showcasing that with the right approach, dreams can indeed come true.

EVERY THING STARTS WITH A DREAM

Take your Dream for a Test Drive!

You've set the scene, built your home, considered work, and thought about your perfect day. Now just like Diego and Riley, it's time to write your story. Start with your vision - the way you'd like to live. Add some bullet points that describe your journey. Finally, write your happy ending. It's time to embrace financial freedom!

Your Vision:

Your Journey:

Your Dream Life:

Identify your Values and Priorities

Financial freedom is not just about accumulating wealth; it's about aligning your finances with your deepest values and priorities. It's a means to an end, a tool to help you live a life that resonates with your values and priorities. Envision your life as a scenic highway, with each of your roadside stops and exciting excursions representing the central pieces that infuse it with meaning and purpose. Financial freedom acts as your trusty road map, guiding you to seamlessly arrange these remarkable experiences into a harmonious and fulfilling journey.

> **"You can afford anything. You just can't afford everything."**
> **- Paula Pant**

In the hustle and bustle of our consumer-driven world, it's alarmingly easy to fall into the trap of mindless spending. We've all been there, making impulse purchases, subscribing to services we rarely use, and accumulating possessions that clutter our lives. In these moments, our financial decisions often lack a clear sense of purpose or alignment with our priorities. It's like driving aimlessly without a map or GPS, unsure of where we're headed or why.

However, there's a powerful shift that occurs when you gain clarity on your values and priorities. It's like discovering the destination of your life's journey. Suddenly, every choice you make, including your financial decisions, becomes intentional and purpose-driven. You begin to discern what truly matters to you, whether it's fostering relationships, pursuing passions, or securing your future. Your values serve as your compass, and financial freedom becomes the vehicle that propels you toward your chosen destinations.

With your values and priorities firmly established, you embark on a path of purposeful action. You no longer succumb to the allure of mindless spending because you understand that every dollar spent is a reflection of your values and an investment in your dream life. Financial decisions become a means to build the life you desire, rather than an obstacle to it. This intentional approach to life, including your finances, leads to a profound sense of fulfillment and empowerment.

What do you Value?

Before we dive into the activity, take a moment to consider the role of values in your pursuit of financial freedom. Your values shape your priorities, influence your goals, and ultimately determine the kind of life you wish to lead. As we explore these values, you'll gain clarity on what truly matters to you, providing a solid foundation for making intentional financial choices that align with your vision of a fulfilling life. So, let's begin by identifying those values that resonate most deeply with you.

Values

Below are 14 common values. **Circle the values** that are most important to you.

Freedom

Health

Creativity

Education

Love

Respect

Family

Community

Honesty

Success

Gratitude

Adventure

Integrity

Compassion

Set Your Priorities

Fantastic job on circling your values! Now, I invite you to embark on a deeper journey by identifying your top priorities. These priorities are the beating heart of your aspirations, the elements of your life that hold the most profound significance. With these priorities in mind, your financial decisions will become intentional, purposeful steps toward the life you've always envisioned. Your priorities will serve as the foundation upon which you build your financial strategy, ensuring that every choice you make is a step closer to the life you desire.

Priority Pyramid Activity

1. Place your most important values at the base of the pyramid. These are the values that are absolutely essential to your sense of self and well-being. Use the values from the previous page, or add your own.
2. Work your way up, placing values that are important but not as central as you go higher.
3. Take a moment to step back and look at your Priority Pyramid. Reflect on the arrangement and make any adjustments you feel are necessary. Your pyramid should be a true reflection of what matters most to you. (See the example on next page.)

Yuki's Priority Pyramid

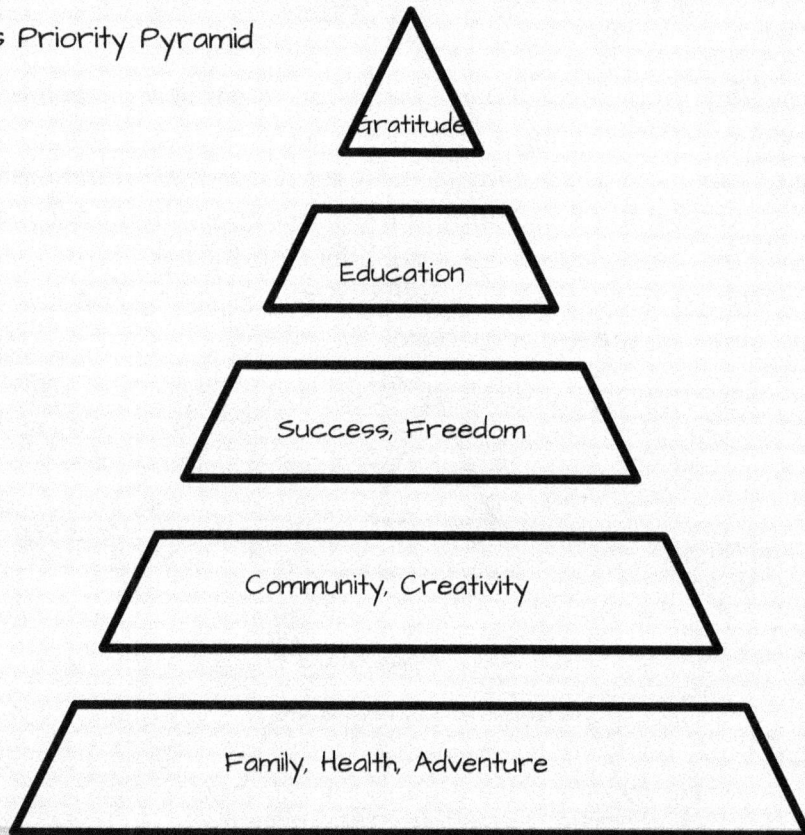

Gratitude

Education

Success, Freedom

Community, Creativity

Family, Health, Adventure

Meet Yuki, a young professional on her journey towards financial freedom. Yuki started this exercise with a long list of values, but as she began to construct her Priority Pyramid, she realized that Family, Health, and Adventure were her foundational values, forming the base of her pyramid. These were the values she couldn't imagine life without.

Moving up the pyramid, Yuki placed Community and Creativity, followed by Success and Freedom. These values represented her aspirations and what she aimed to achieve on her path to financial freedom. Next, she recognized her desire to learn, and added Education in the fourth tier. Finally, at the top of her pyramid, she placed Gratitude, a reminder of the importance of appreciating every step of her journey.

Yuki's Priority Pyramid was a vivid pictorial representation of her core values and priorities. It served as a reminder of what truly mattered to her. With financial freedom in mind, Yuki tailored her financial decisions to ensure they were in harmony with her pyramid. She discovered that by aligning her financial choices with her values, she not only reached her financial goals, but also felt a deeper sense of fulfillment and purpose.

Financial Freedom Means . . .

Your destination is financial freedom. You painted the canvas of your dream life, each brushstroke reflecting the vivid colors of your deepest desires. You identified your values and priorities, shaping the compass that guides you through the financial landscape. Now, it's time for you to write down what financial freedom means to you.

Financial Freedom Means . . .

Examples

Financial freedom means I can travel and explore the world, immersing myself in diverse cultures and experiences.

Financial freedom means I can live in the place that truly makes my heart sing, surrounded by the serenity and beauty that I've handpicked for my ideal life.

Financial freedom means I have the flexibility to spend quality time with my loved ones and create awesome memories.

Financial freedom means I can support causes and organizations that align with my values and make a positive impact on the world.

Financial freedom means I can break free from the cycle of debt and finally stop worrying about money.

Financial freedom means that I can live my life on my own terms, with the freedom to define success and happiness in ways that bring me joy.

AWESOME!

Hey, you did it! Great job on completing this awesome chapter and building out your dream life. I'm super excited about the future ahead of you! Here's what you should have discovered.

☐ You have a totally amazing dream life that will drive your journey. It is uniquely yours and you can't wait to get started!

You've come a long way! When you started our Road Trip, you weren't sure of your destination. Now you have a clear picture of your destination. You have set the scene, created your home, figured out how work fits in, and thought about your perfect day. You began to explore the journey that might take you to your dream life. This is nothing short of spectacular!

☐ You know your values. Your priorities are set and you can now take actions - physically, mentally, emotionally, and financially - that feed your priorities.

The best road trip is the one that travels at your pace and excites your sense of adventure. Some people are driven to drive as fast as they can to reach their destination. Others enjoy the scenic route and treasure those unusual roadside stops along the way. The journey is yours to travel. Let your values and priorities guide you on your route.

☐ You know what financial freedom means to you!

Here's the best part: You are clear on what financial freedom means to you. And this, my friend, is what will drive you to great heights. You know that financial freedom goes well beyond money. In fact, money is nothing more than a tool . . . the most amazing tool ever invented that will help you build the life of your dreams.

Financial freedom is the journey that allows you to turn our dreams into reality while staying true to your core values and priorities. The road ahead is bright, and with every step you take, you move closer to your destination: freedom.

Notes

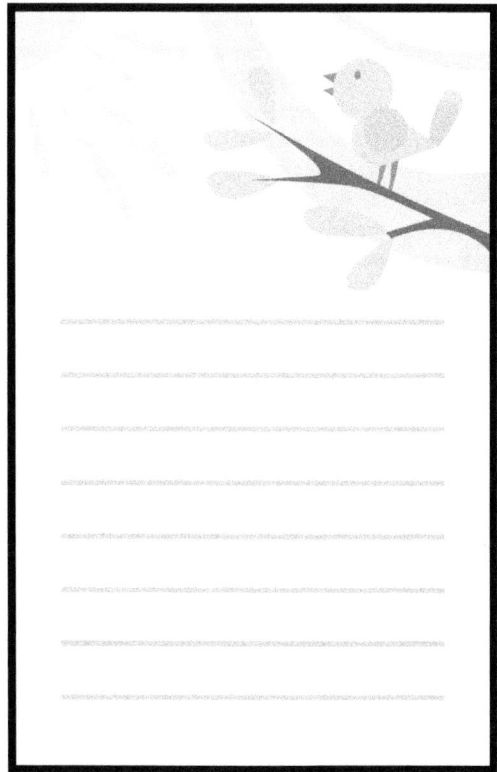

3

LIGHTEN YOUR LOAD

Lighten Your Load

The lighter you pack, the faster you travel! In this chapter, you get the chance to pause, take a deep breath, and reassess the baggage you're carrying on this road trip. It's time to unpack the excess luggage that only drags you down. Make room for a brighter, more empowered mindset.

Objectives

- To discover your money mindset and personality
- To gain a deeper understanding of your financial past
- To strengthen your relationship with money

Big Mission

Our mission is to help you shed the baggage that no longer serves you and pave the way for a refreshed and empowered financial mindset.

To-do Checklist

- ☐ Take the money personality quiz
- ☐ Record your money highs and lows
- ☐ Write a love letter to money!

Discover your Money Mindset and Personality

In the world of road trips, there's a golden rule: pack lightly! For this particular journey, I'm challenging you to fit everything into a trusty backpack. It might seem like a daunting task, but I have full faith in your abilities!

Now, let's talk about the baggage we're addressing here. This isn't the kind you toss into your car, but the experiences and relationships that have profoundly influenced the way you perceive money. Think of this baggage as the "excess" weight, those things that burden your mind and occasionally sabotage your best intentions.

Consider, for a moment, what you learned about money during your formative years. Were you equipped with the knowledge and confidence to build wealth, or were you handed the age-old adage that money can't buy happiness? Do you find yourself lugging around the weight of past experiences that hinder your progress toward your financial aspirations? It's time to unpack those bags, clear the mental clutter, and embark on this financial journey with a lighter load and a brighter outlook.

Select your Luggage

Which image best describes the financial baggage you are carrying? Shade the button that describes you best.

O	O	O
I have some decent money habits and the support and tools I need to be successful.	I have some money hang-ups that will take some work to overcome. But I know I can do it.	I learned a lot of negative things about money. This might be tough, but I'm up for it!

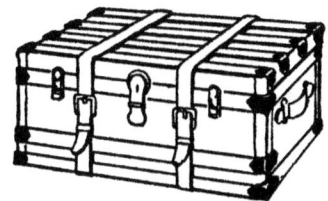

The Secret World of Money

Money. It's a word that determines the quality of our lives, but most of us aren't taught about money. It's conspicuously absent from our educational system, or it's taught in such a way that it makes us want to drive our car off a cliff! It's as if we're handed the keys to a car but never taught how to drive it. And that's where the problem begins.

So most of us start our financial journey without a map, and it's easy to get lost - or never start our route. Worse, we don't have a navigator who can give us directions. Money is taboo; it's a secret that is whispered about behind closed doors. The message is clear: money is not to be discussed. This silence around money creates a veil of mystery, one that often leads to uninformed choices and deep-rooted misconceptions about finances.

It's not our fault if we come into this journey with a giant suitcase of lousy habits and poor decisions. The money mindset we carry, the beliefs and behaviors that shape our financial decisions, are not inherently our own. Instead, they're a patchwork quilt woven from the observations we've made throughout our lives. We've learned about money by watching our families, friends, and even society at large.

The way our parents handled money, the tales of financial triumphs and setbacks among our friends, the glimpses of opulence and frugality portrayed in the media—all these elements silently etch into our minds, creating the blueprint of our money mindset. It's a mindset that often leads us down a path paved with habits, beliefs, and assumptions, some of which may not serve our best interests.

Circle the face that best represents your experience

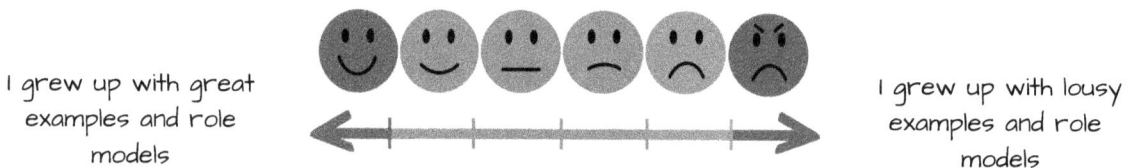

I grew up with great examples and role models

I grew up with lousy examples and role models

But here's the empowering truth: we have the power to change the way we think about money. We can rewrite the script that's been passed down through generations. We can break free from the shackles of silent lessons and step into the light of financial empowerment. It all begins with understanding our money personality, and how we can strengthen our mindset to go after our dreams.

While we might be starting our journey with a heavy load, there's a powerful force that we can use to our advantage. It's our money mindset—an intricate web of beliefs, attitudes, and behaviors that guide our relationship with money. It's the lens through which we view financial opportunities, the filter that shapes our financial choices, and the hidden architect behind the financial reality we create for ourselves. Our money mindset, much like the compass on a road trip, directs our financial journey, whether we're consciously aware of it or not.

"Your mindset is the lens through which you view the world. Change the lens, and you change your life."
- Carol Dweck

Get Better Mileage with an Abundance Mindset

Abundance Mindset

An **abundance** mindset is characterized by a positive and optimistic view of money and finances. Those with an abundance mindset believe that there are ample opportunities to earn, save, and invest money. They focus on possibilities and see setbacks as temporary challenges to overcome. People with this mindset tend to be more open to taking calculated risks to achieve financial success. They often have a proactive approach to money management and believe in their ability to create wealth.

Scarcity Mindset

A **scarcity** mindset is rooted in fear and a belief that there is a limited amount of money available. Individuals with a scarcity mindset often worry about running out of money, struggle with financial anxiety, and may be hesitant to invest or take financial risks. They tend to focus on limitations, view money as a source of stress, and may have difficulty breaking free from financial patterns that perpetuate scarcity.

Let's take a closer look at our two mindsets. You might be fully locked into an abundance or scarcity mindset - or you might share outlooks from both types. For example, Tonya has an unwavering belief in her ability to create wealth and achieve financial success. She approaches investment opportunities with optimism and has diversified her portfolio to maximize potential returns. Despite her financial accomplishments, Tonya struggles with the fear of running out of money. She often hesitates to spend on personal enjoyment or treats herself because she's worried about potential future financial setbacks. Where are you on the abundance/scarcity scale?.

Table of Abundance and Scarcity Traits
Shade the buttons below that best describe your money mindset.

	Abundance	Scarcity	
O	Embraces opportunities and believes in ample possibilities for financial success.	Views opportunities as limited, often missing out on potential gains due to fear or hesitation.	O
O	Sees setbacks as temporary challenges to overcome and learn from.	Perceives setbacks as insurmountable obstacles, leading to a sense of helplessness.	O
O	Views money as a tool to create a fulfilling life and make a positive impact.	Views money as a source of stress and anxiety, leading to a constant focus on financial limitations.	O
O	Willing to take calculated risks to achieve financial goals and explore new ventures.	Reluctant to take financial risks, preferring the safety of familiar financial habits.	O

Do you lean toward the abundance mindset? Or perhaps the scarcity mindset? Remember, this is your starting point. If you want to build a better relationship with money - and power up your abundance mindset - you can do it! You will have to be intentional with your actions and learn to embrace possibilities, overcome fear, and cultivate a positive relationship with money.

Keisha's story began in a modest neighborhood where she grew up with her single mother, who worked tirelessly to make ends meet. Financial conversations were often laced with anxiety and tension, leading young Keisha to internalize a scarcity mindset. The message was clear: money was scarce, and one must hoard it to survive. This mindset became her guiding light through early adulthood.

A turning point arrived when Keisha encountered a mentor at a community event who spoke passionately about the power of education and investing. Intrigued, Keisha decided to explore further. She began attending financial literacy workshops and devouring books on personal finance. Slowly but surely, her mindset started to shift.

Keisha's first step toward abundance was education. She enrolled in online classes to earn her degree while working full-time during the day. It was challenging, but she was determined to invest in her future. This step was pivotal in challenging the notion that she was limited by her background.

As her confidence grew, Keisha made her first foray into the world of investments. She started small, carefully researching stocks and mutual funds. Her early investments showed modest returns, but Keisha didn't falter. She saw them as valuable learning experiences, gradually shedding the fear of losing money.

Keisha's journey toward an abundance mindset wasn't just about finances—it was about embracing the abundance of life itself. She joined a community group that supported personal growth, where she learned the importance of gratitude and saw the opportunities surrounding her.

Over the years, Keisha's mindset continued to transform. She started a small business, leveraged her investments, and even ventured into philanthropy. The once-scared girl who believed money was scarce had blossomed into a woman who saw opportunities everywhere she looked. Keisha 's scarcity mindset had given way to a profound sense of abundance.

Today, Keisha is a vivid example of an abundance mindset. Her financial stability and success are products of her journey from scarcity to abundance. She not only invests wisely but also nurtures her relationships, her community, and her dreams with boundless optimism. Keisha 's story is a testament to the transformative power of mindset and determination in the pursuit of financial freedom and personal growth.

Remember, your mindset is not carved in stone. You have the incredible ability to reshape your mindset and transform your life. While understanding your mindset is crucial, an even more enlightening compass is your unique money personality. This insightful tool unveils your personal relationship with finances and equips you with tailored strategies for success. To discover your money personality, I've crafted an enjoyable quiz consisting of just five simple questions. Are you a Voyager, Scout, Wanderer, or Globetrotter? Let's embark on this fun exploration together!

Take the Money Personality Quiz

Use the link or scan the barcode to take the quiz. Then shade the button that corresponds to your results.

bit.ly/drbmoneyquiz

Voyagers

VOYAGERS prepare and plan for the long journey ahead. They focus on the destination and are fully capable of overcoming any obstacles in their path.

Voyagers are incredibly organized and disciplined. There's something about the process of planning that gives them pleasure. But sometimes . . . they are so focused on work that they forget to dream. Maybe it's time to shift gears and think of wealth as an abundance of time? How would that change your perspective?

Key Challenge

You're so busy being responsible and planning for the future, that you're neglecting to have fun today.

Try this Affirmation

I choose to invest in my own time and happiness

Scouts

SCOUTS look out for others. Their job is to find safe passage for those who follow.

You are a born saver! Dependable and responsible are your middle names. You love helping others and making their day. But underneath your generosity is an undercurrent of worry. You're afraid of taking risks, but you know you have to make wiser decisions with your money. And if you keep putting everyone else's needs first, you might not have enough money to enjoy your later years.

Key Challenge

You've pushed your own joy - and needs - to the back of the line.

Try this Affirmation

I am worth investing in my own future.

Wanderers

WANDERERS love an open road and all day to explore. They prefer to travel without maps and guides, letting the winds take them where they may.

You are a free spirit. You're loaded with creativity and you embrace the bright colors of life. You are passionate about your beliefs and the way you live. But somewhere deep inside, you believe that there's something "wrong" with having money. It just doesn't fit with your free spirit approach to living.

Key Challenge

You have negative thoughts about money and how it might ruin your creativity and free spirit.

Try this Affirmation

Money supports my happiness. I can use it to spread joy.

Globetrotters

GLOBETROTTERS seek experiences from every corner of the world. They love the idea of new places and new faces and find friends wherever they go.

Underneath your fun-loving personality is a more complex person. You have a "live for today" mantra, but deep down inside, you worry about tomorrow. What if it all comes crashing down? Still, you resist taking responsibility for your money, and your future.

Key Challenge

You love all the things that money can buy, but you hate being the one responsible for earning and tracking it.

Try this Affirmation

I can afford anything. I just can't afford everything.

Now that you've taken a moment to reflect on your mindset and your money personality, have you recognized how this information can serve as a guiding compass on your road trip, steering you towards smooth terrain, or potentially leading to a flat tire on a dark, deserted highway? As you continue your journey, I encourage you to nurture inner strength, for the knowledge you've gained about your mindset and personality tendencies is nothing short of a superpower.

But how do you harness this newfound superpower and transform into your own financial superhero? The key lies in your self-awareness—your understanding of your thoughts, behaviors, and, ultimately, your habits. To guide you on this path, here are three superhero traits that will help you on your journey Where do you find yourself on each of these dimensions?

Shade in the circle that best describes you!

Mindful Actions - Mindfulness is a superpower in its own right. Be aware of your intentions and how your actions align with your values and goals. Pause before reacting to your emotions.

O ——— O ——— O ——— O ——— O

I need help   That's me!

Superhero Friends - Every superhero needs superhero friends to defeat the villains. Surround yourself with positivity. Don't let your detractors bring you down.

O ——— O ——— O ——— O ——— O

I need help   That's me!

Gratitude - Superheroes know they have been given unique gifts that must be put to good use. They recognize the importance of the people around them and the environment in which they live. They practice gratitude on a daily basis.

O ——— O ——— O ——— O ——— O

I need help   That's me!

Here's a universal truth about life: STUFF HAPPENS! There are moments when your mindset, personality, and even your actions may not seem enough to navigate the storm. But here's what I want you to acknowledge within yourself - your RESILIENCE! You see, this road trip we're embarking on will encounter road construction, detours, and bad weather. In preparation for the unknown, I invite you to take a journey back in time. Trust me; you'll discover that your strength surpasses your own expectations

Gain a Deeper Understanding of your Financial Past

Money. It flows in and out of our lives, doesn't it? We've all experienced those moments when we felt like financial kings and queens, and other times when we feared a lifetime of financial struggles. It's time to revisit your money highlights - those glorious times when money seemed to fall from the heavens - and the lowlights - those challenging moments when storm clouds threatened to divert your path.

Before you dive into this exercise, take a moment to sit back and reflect on your past. No need to pass judgment on the events that unfolded; after all, you can't change the past. Instead, view your money stories as if you were an impartial observer. Consider it a narrative, an integral part of what has shaped you into the person you are today. To get you started, here's an example that should kickstart the process.

Alyx's Money Highs and Lows

Alyx is on a mission to understand their financial history, one step at a time. They know that this approach will give them a much-broader perspective of their journey to financial freedom. And it will demonstrate their own resilience and determination.

Money Highlights

They reflected on significant moments where they excelled financially. These highlights included successfully saving for a dream vacation, receiving a surprise bonus at work, mastering the art of budgeting to pay off student loans faster, and becoming a confident investor. Their biggest highlight? Negotiating a big raise following an exemplary performance review.

Money Lowlights

It wasn't difficult remembering the pain they felt during financial hard times. The unexpected medical bill following a trip to the emergency room was still raw. Alyx recalled other lowlights - the time they loaned money to a friend (and never got it back), the credit card debt after a wild road trip with friends. Then there's the house they recently bought and the unexpected surprises, like the broken A/C. Despite all those events, they will never forget their stint of unemployment. Not only did they drain their savings, but they lost confidence. It was the most challenging time of their life.

Alyx's Enlightened Perspective

As Alyx progressed through their money timeline journey, they started to see the bigger picture. The combination of highlights and lowlights revealed that the road to financial freedom was indeed a winding one. They understood that financial setbacks were not failures but rather opportunities for growth and learning. Armed with this newfound perspective, Alyx discovered that every experience, positive or negative, contributed to their financial wisdom.

Alyx's Money Stories

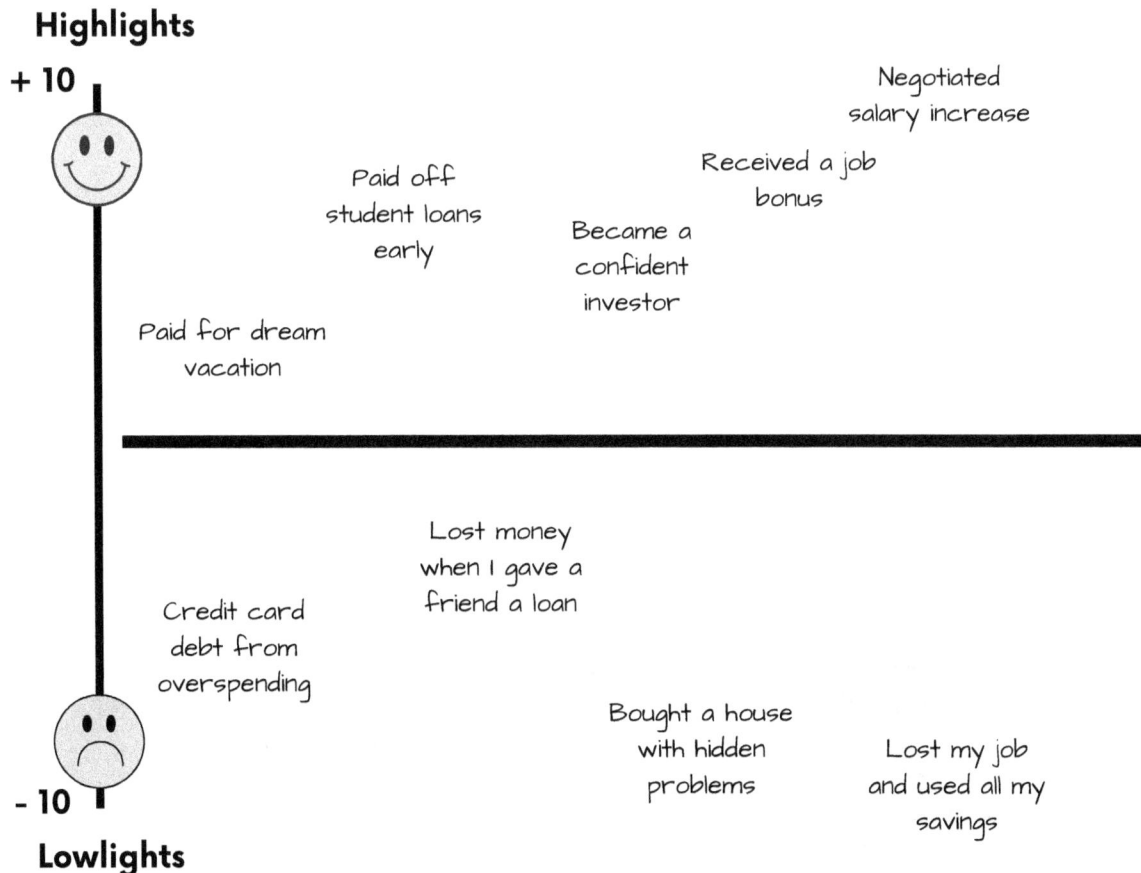

Highlights

+ 10

Negotiated salary increase

Paid off student loans early

Received a job bonus

Became a confident investor

Paid for dream vacation

Lost money when I gave a friend a loan

Credit card debt from overspending

Bought a house with hidden problems

Lost my job and used all my savings

- 10

Lowlights

Now it's your time to shine. Add your own money highlights and lowlights to the chart below. When you've completed it, take a few moments to gaze upon your journey. What revelations have surfaced? Did this exercise stir emotions that were tucked away? Can you now appreciate the incredible resilience that has propelled you to this point? That same resilience will be your guiding force moving forward.

My Money Stories

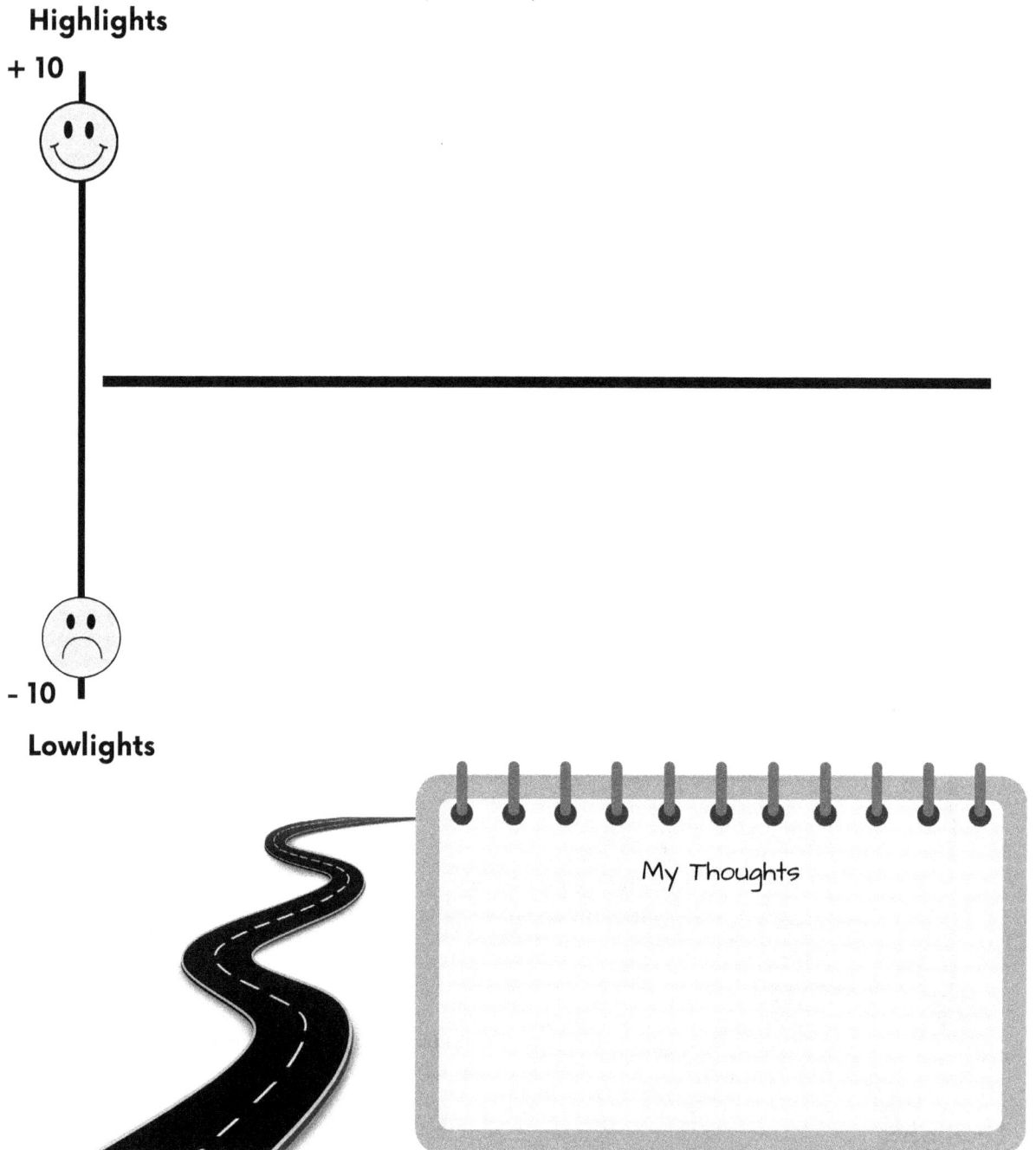

Highlights

+ 10

- 10

Lowlights

My Thoughts

Strengthen your Relationship with Money

I am genuinely proud of you! I can sense those layers of unnecessary baggage shedding away, leaving you nearly at backpack size. Just one more activity before we fire up the engine for our road trip. By now, your relationship with money should be a keen focus of your awareness. You've journeyed through moments of prosperity and adversity. Today, it's about embracing the present and envisioning the future. It's time to bid farewell to the less desirable aspects of your relationship. It's time to craft a love letter!

What do you write in a love letter? On the following page, you can read my own letter as an example. Then, it's your turn to compose your own. I'll tell you this – my letter carries a touch of pain, because my financial past has seen its share of hardships. But writing my love letter was a cathartic experience. It allowed me to release pent-up emotions and left me feeling empowered for the journey ahead. I want the same for you. Now isn't the time to hold back your emotions. This letter is uniquely yours. It's an intimate expression, deeply personal, and profoundly powerful.

⚠️ **HAZARD: Put your judgement aside. You CAN fall in love!**

Approach this assignment with an open heart. Now is the perfect moment to adopt the abundance mindset and consider how your money personality may have influenced your relationship with finances. There are two things to keep in mind as you embark on this assignment:

☐ **JUDGING** - Set aside your inner critic. We've all made mistakes, and life doesn't always unfold as we envisioned. Resist the urge to blame yourself or others. Instead, take a step back and narrate your story. Pour your emotions into this letter without judgment.

☐ **RELUCTANCE** - You might hesitate to express your affection for money, especially if you lean towards being a Wanderer. Release that reluctance. Understand that money has the potential to open doors, bring joy, and lead you to your dream life. It's time to wholeheartedly embrace your relationship with money!

♥♥♥♥♥♥

Dear Money,

Gosh, we have a twisted relationship. When I was younger, I had to work hard to get your attention. I remember spending my teenage years baling hay on the farm. Dad paid me a penny a bale. A good day was $10 in my pocket. I learned that the more I worked, the more I could get paid. I believed that the quality of my work mattered. I believed in the American dream.

But money, you wrecked our relationship in my early 30s. I've never been the same. I did all the right things. I finished my doctoral degree. I published my dissertation as a book. I did a stint as an adjunct faculty. And yet, you abandoned me, and I lost all hope. You broke me.

It took me five states and more than three years before we were reunited. And it was a fabulous reunion. But I never trusted you. I put half of your paychecks aside for the future, because I didn't want to be dependent on you ever again. I saved and learned how to invest, so that our relationship would become healthy.

And then . . . the unimaginable happened. My career suddenly ended. And our relationship moved into another phase. You gave me the freedom to shift to a new career, and I thank you for that. But truthfully, those early days still hurt me. I worry and fear more than I should. And I'm tired of it.

Money, I've learned to love you, even with all your faults. I'm ready to release the anger and disappointment you've brought into my life. Because Money, as I write this, I am watching the sun rise over the ocean. You have helped me turn my life into the most amazing adventure. You've helped me erase the wrinkles and stress that came with my old career. I feel so damn good about our future together.

Money, I love you. Thank you for the way you have allowed me to bring joy into my world. Thank you for giving me the opportunity to discover who I am. Thank you for all the amazing sunrises and sunsets I've witnessed from magical corners of the world. Thank you for helping me raise my son, and for allowing me to take good care of my cat companions.

I know you're not perfect. Neither am I. But we're good together. I can't wait to see what our next adventure might entail. I love you!

Brenda

Dear Money,

AWESOME!

Wow, once again, an incredible effort on your part! Can you sense the difference? You've just shed a load of baggage that was dragging you down. Here's what you should have uncovered.

☐ You gained a profound understanding of your money mindset and personality, and how they shape your thoughts and actions when it comes to finances.

By unveiling the intricacies of your money mindset and personality, you now have a powerful compass to navigate the financial landscapes of your life. You're better poised to make deliberate choices and align your financial decisions with your values and priorities. Embrace this newfound awareness as you continue on your road trip to financial freedom, for it will be your faithful guide in the journey ahead.

☐ You are resilient. Your reflection on your money highs and lows has reinforced your inner strength.

By writing down the highlights and lowlights of your financial journey, you've unearthed a remarkable truth about yourself—your innate resilience. Your experiences serve as a testament to your capacity to overcome obstacles and adapt to the ever-changing landscape of life. You are stepping forward into this journey with unwavering confidence, knowing that you have what it takes to be successful.

☐ You laid the groundwork for a thriving and harmonious relationship with money. Congratulations!

As you nurture this newfound love and understanding of money, you've forged a solid foundation for a prosperous and fulfilling financial journey. Your dedication to building a healthier relationship with your finances sets the stage for a brighter and more secure future.

You've diligently shed the baggage that was weighing you down, a remarkable achievement. Your path to financial freedom has just received a turbo boost. Well done!

Notes

4

MAP YOUR ROUTE

Map your Route

Let's talk about your route to financial freedom. In this chapter, we'll explore just how much you need to reach financial freedom and create a roadmap to track your progress.. And we'll set up mile markers so you can gauge your progress. Let's GPS this trip!

Objectives

- To discover how much money you need
- To know your starting point - your net worth
- To create mile markers (goals)

Big Mission

Our mission is to help you create your very own roadmap to financial freedom.

To-do Checklist

☐ Estimate your "magic" numbers

☐ Know your starting point

☐ Set your priorities

We Need Some Tunes!

Welcome to the heart of our Money Road Trip adventure - we're about to map your route. We've got a thrilling journey ahead, so before you fasten your seatbelt, how about crafting a playlist that'll keep your spirits high? Get ready to groove as we rev up for the adventure of a lifetime!

Need some inspiration? Explore these tracks, and then get ready to build your very own playlist. Let's get the wheels turning and rock this journey!

♫♫♫♫♫♫♫♫♫♫♫♫

I Won't Back Down" by Tom Petty
"Try Everything" by Shakira
"Don't Stop Believin'" by Journey
"Fight Song" by Rachel Platten
"The Climb" by Miley Cyrus
"Rise," by Katy Perry

My Road Trip Playlist

_____

_____

_____

_____

_____

_____

_____

Discover How Much Money You Need

Have you ever gone on a road trip with a crew of diverse personalities? Imagine hitting the open road with that one friend who guarantees a journey filled with excitement (and possibly a hefty price tag). Now, picture yourself with a more serious friend, whose primary focus is on reaching your destination efficiently, without unnecessary diversions. Remember those distinct money personalities we explored in the previous chapter? Well, it's time to introduce our companions for this ride, the Globetrotter and the Voyager, and see how they prefer to spend their money.

Our Globetrotter has a taste for luxury. We call them "Luxe Lexi." Lexi's idea of a road trip involves five-star hotels with room service, gourmet meals, and exclusive spa treatments. They purchased and shipped an antique suit of armor that "spoke" to them at the roadside flea market. Every stop is a chance is to purchase more "treasures."

Our Voyager is our practical and down-to-earth traveler. Let's call him "Practical Pete." Pete is all about affordable motels and cozy Airbnb rentals. He finds joy in local diners and homemade meals on the road. His entertainment includes scenic hikes, stargazing, and free roadside attractions. Pete knows how to make the most of every dollar.

Alright, let's get down to business! That snazzy suit of armor? It's not a necessity, it's a pure indulgence that could seriously dent your finances. It's time to take a magnifying glass to your spending habits. Ask yourself a crucial question: Am I spending money on things that I genuinely need, or is it because I want them at that moment?

Now, let's dive deep into the financial details. I'm challenging you to review your expenses over the past 30 days, and if possible, stretch it to 60 days. You can either use the form on the next page or rely on your preferred budgeting tool, software, or app. But here's the twist – as you dissect your spending, add this critical layer: Was this purchase a fundamental need or a tempting want?

Your values come into play, too. Take a gym membership, for instance. It's a necessity if it aligns with your health and you're a regular gym visitor. However, it drifts into the want realm if it's more of a well-intentioned idea while your gym visits remain sporadic. And when it comes to dining out, indulging from time to time is delightful, but take a moment to ponder if that restaurant meal is a daily ritual when you could whip up a nutritious, homemade meal. Here's the challenge: be brutally honest with yourself - is it a genuine need?

EXPENSE TRACKER FOR MONTH OF _____

Directions: Record all of your expenses for the last 30 days (preferably 60 days). Make extra copies - or use your own spreadsheets, software, or apps.

Examples of **categories** include rent, mortgage, groceries, dining out, auto loan, fuel, necessities, clothing, pet supplies, health care, entertainment, housewares, childcare, etc.

DATE	DESCRIPTION	CATEGORY	AMOUNT	WANT OR NEED?
				W / N
				W / N
				W / N
				W / N
				W / N
				W / N
				W / N
				W / N
				W / N
				W / N
				W / N
				W / N
				W / N
				W / N
				W / N
				W / N
				W / N
				W / N

TOTAL

How did this exercise sit with you? Let's be real; this is where emotions can sometimes throw a wrench into our best-laid plans. Last month, maybe you weren't at the top of your game when it came to spending. You had a couple of rough days at work, and you filled up your Amazon shopping cart more than you intended. Or perhaps your fluffy cat needed a visit to the vet, and an unexpected bill hit you. Life has a way of serving up these curveballs to all of us.

Now, when it comes to taking the reins of your finances and paving the road to financial freedom, intentionality is your trusty co-pilot. But here's the deal - we're all carting around a load of baggage when it comes to our money, and that can make it tricky to take a step back and get a clear view of what's really going on. You've logged your numbers and facts, but there's more beneath the surface. Let's roll up our sleeves and dig into those numbers.

My total monthly expenses (if you recorded expenses over two months, divide that total amount by two)

_____

I spent this much money on NEEDS   _____

I spent this much money on WANTS   _____

The percentage of the Total I spent on NEEDS:

_____%

The percentage of the Total I spent on WANTS:

_____%

This is how I feel about my spending habits: (circle one)

Let's head back to the million-dollar question: How much money do you need for your road trip to financial freedom? Well, it all depends on the wheels you choose, where you lay your head at night, and what adventures you have in store. Imagine three distinct vehicles, each representing different lifestyles. The first, an eco-friendly hybrid car symbolizes a frugal and eco-conscious approach. Next up, a trusty sedan embodies a middle-of-the-road, comfortable lifestyle. Lastly, a swanky sports car, signifies a lavish and extravagant journey.

FRUGAL
You believe in value and aren't into excessive consumption

COMFORTABLE
You have everything you need and can afford occasional splurges

LUXURIOUS
You like the high-end goods and the status that comes with luxury brands

Based on your current average monthly expenses, <u>estimate</u> about how much money you would need each month for a frugal, comfortable, or luxurious lifestyle.

	Frugal	Comfortable	Luxurious
Estimated Monthly Expenses	_____	_____	_____

Take a look at the triangle on the following page. At the base, we have Financial Security, represented by having one year's worth of expenses saved up. At the pinnacle sits Financial Independence, where you've accumulated 25 times your annual expenses, making work optional. Now, nestled in between these two, we find Financial Freedom, a delightful zone where you can comfortably take some risks and chase your dreams.

Here are the instructions for using the triangle graphic:
1. Enter your monthly estimates for each of the three lifestyles on the first line below the triangle graphic.
2. Multiply each monthly estimate by 12 to calculate your expected annual expenses, which represents your financial security level.
3. Take that annual expenses number (your financial security number), and multiply it by 25. This will give you your financial independence number that signifies when you can live off your savings and investments, making work optional.

Financial Security, Freedom, and Independence

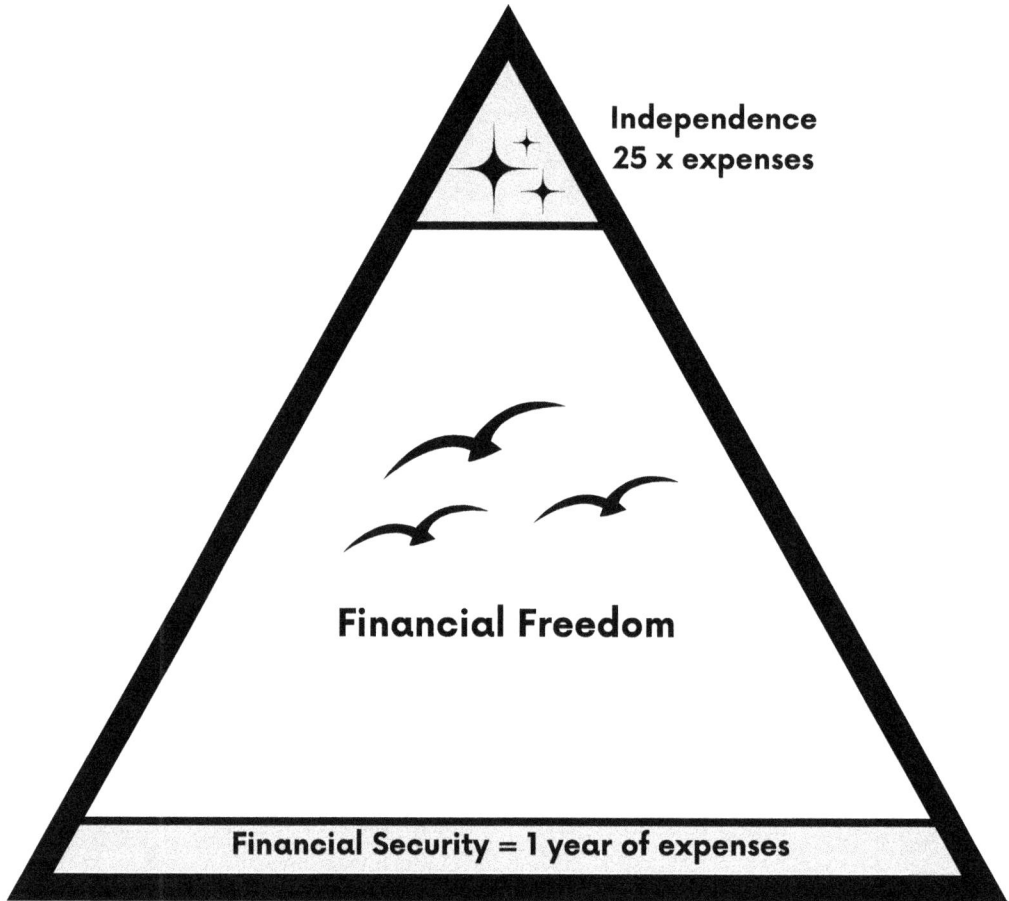

Independence
25 x expenses

Financial Freedom

Financial Security = 1 year of expenses

Estimated Expenses

	Frugal	Comfortable	Luxurious
Monthly Expenses	_____	_____	_____
Financial Security (Monthly Expenses x 12)	_____	_____	_____
Independence (Financial Security x 25)	_____	_____	_____

Are you feeling sticker shock? It's okay! Don't throw this Workbook at the dog. Take a look at the different amounts of money you need for a frugal versus luxurious lifestyle. It's perfectly cool to start with the frugal number. Once you've reached that goal, you can work your way up to the higher levels. Now I think it's storytime to show you how this might work. Let's bring back Luxe Lexi and Practical Pete.

Lexi's High-Flying Luxurious Life

Meet Luxe Lexi, an individual who knows how to savor the finer things in life. Lexi resides in a lavish penthouse apartment, drives a high-end sports car and has an affinity for haute couture fashion. Combined with their penchant for fine dining and travels to exotic destinations several times a year, their monthly expenses average $21,000. Let's run their numbers:

Financial Security: $21,000 x 12 = $252,000
Financial Independence: $252,000 x 25 = $6,300,000
Financial Freedom Range: $252,001 - $6,299,999

Pete's Practical Lifestyle

Now, let's look a little deeper into Practical Pete's expenses. He has a modest apartment, drives an older sedan, and works remotely as much as the company allows. This helps him keep his transportation, clothing, and food expenses low. Pete values health and fitness and values his gym membership. He prefers local adventures and finds bargain travel deals for his occasional vacations. Pete spends about $4,000 per month.

Financial Security: $4,000 x 12 = $48,000
Financial Independence: $48,000 x 25 = $1,200,000
Financial Freedom Range: $48,001 - $1,199,999

Now, set your sights on your immediate financial goal: achieving financial security. But hold onto your hats because we're not stopping there – we're aiming for the sweet spot known as financial freedom. The road to financial independence may seem like a daunting journey, which is precisely why we're honing in on financial freedom. This milestone is within your grasp, offering a broad spectrum to aim for – some may embrace freedom after they've saved up a year's worth of expenses, while others may prefer to have a safety net that spans ten or more years. The choice is entirely yours!

I have unwavering belief in your ability to conquer this journey. As you make smart financial decisions and fine-tune your lifestyle, you're not just on the road to financial freedom – you're cruising towards it with confidence. Remember, you possess the power to transform your financial future. Keep your eyes on the horizon, and remain vigilant against these two potential roadblocks that may try to divert your financial journey. You've got this!

☐ **IMPATIENCE** - Buckle up, my friend, because this journey is a marathon, not a sprint. Unless you hit the jackpot, reaching your financial goals will likely take years of dedication and effort. Plus, the financial markets can be quite the rollercoaster. Be patient, and your persistence will eventually reap great rewards.

☐ **LIFESTYLE CREEP** - The biggest roadside robber is lifestyle creep. Just when you feel like you've tamed your expenses, a promotion, a hefty bonus, or a significant income boost might tempt you into thinking you deserve a more luxurious lifestyle. Luxe Lexi's extravagance can be alluring, but it's vital to stay committed to your financial goals. Make mindful choices about your lifestyle to keep you on the right path.

The future is uncertain. Our financial independence number relies on historical stock market returns and inflation rates. It operates on the assumption that you can safely withdraw 4% of your funds annually without risking depletion. However, some opt for a more cautious approach, using a 3% withdrawal rate (which translates to multiplying your annual expenses by 33 instead of 25).

Know your Starting Point

Remember that playlist you created? It's time to turn up the volume on your favorite tunes! You've done an excellent job estimating your monthly expenses and gaining a clear understanding of the money required to sprinkle the magic of financial freedom into your life. But why do I sense a hint of uncertainty creeping into your brilliant mind?

Let's talk about wealth. It's like a captivating illusion, where appearances can be deceiving. Take Luxe Lexi, for instance. A glimpse at their luxurious penthouse and designer wardrobe might lead you to believe they've got it all figured out in the wealth department. But what if they're concealing a mountain of debt and teetering on the brink of having their credit cards canceled?

Then there's Practical Pete. He doesn't flaunt his wealth and doesn't exude an aura of affluence. His tastes are modest, and he diligently pays off his credit card bills each month. At first glance, Pete may not strike you as wealthy, but the truth is, he's worth far more than our opulent friend Lexi.

If those penthouse suites and luxury cars don't quite cut it as true measures of wealth, what does? Well, I'm delighted you brought that up because the answer is simple yet profound: NET WORTH!

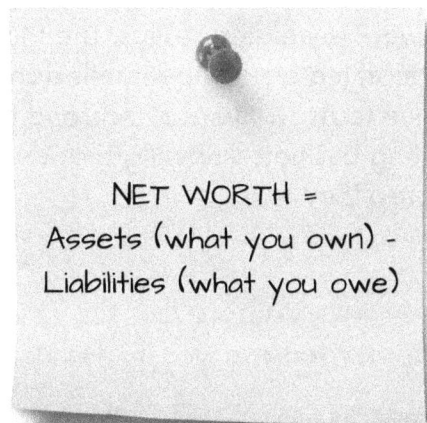

money
IS NOT
Everything
BUT
EVERYTHING
Requires
money

NET WORTH =
Assets (what you own) -
Liabilities (what you owe)

Here's what I love about net worth - it reveals how much you genuinely own once you subtract what you owe. It stands as the ultimate measure of wealth, providing an accurate reflection of your financial health. And, it demonstrates that individuals like Practical Pete can outpace the Luxe Lexis of the world!

The Martinez Family is on a Mission!

In a quiet neighborhood, the Martinez family is on a mission to achieve financial freedom. Lisa Martinez, a devoted stay-at-home mom, and Juan Martinez, an IT professional, are raising their two school-age children, Emily and Miguel.

Lisa, determined to contribute to the family's financial goals while caring for their children, transformed her passion for crafting into a lucrative side hustle. She began crafting and selling handmade jewelry online, not only expressing her creativity but also bolstering the family's income.

Lisa, with her business acumen, assumed the role of the family's financial guru. She immersed himself in financial literature and investment strategies, crafting a diversified portfolio that includes low-cost index funds and individual stocks. Together, they meticulously track their income and expenses, prioritizing savings for emergencies, retirement, education, and a dream fund. Plus, they chipped away at debt, paying off Juan's student loan early and steering clear of credit card debt.

Crucially, the Martinez family remains committed to a frugal lifestyle, eschewing the allure of extravagant homes or flashy cars. Their cozy home and practical vehicles perfectly suit their needs. It allows them to save a high percentage of their income, while still enjoying vacations and family outings.

Their hard work is yielding results. The Martinez family's net worth has now surpassed $300,000, marking a significant milestone on their journey toward financial freedom. They continue to grow their savings and explore Juan's aspiration of establishing his own consulting business, knowing that their financial future is becoming more secure with each step they take.

How committed are you to financial freedom? Rate your dedication level.

| Not Committed | Somewhat Committed | Moderately Committed | Committed | Fully Committed |

My Net Worth Statement

Date: _____

The moment has arrived! Your net worth is your current checkpoint on this journey. Remember, it's just a snapshot in time. No need for self-judgment or dwelling on regrets here. It's all about the numbers. List each asset/liability and its value.

Assets (the stuff I own)

Bank accounts, money markets, CDs, etc.	
	S
	S
	S
	S
Subtotal	S

Taxable accounts (stocks, bonds, etc.)	
	S
	S
	S
	S
Subtotal	S

Retirement accounts	
	S
	S
	S
	S
Subtotal	S

Tax-deferred annuities/life insurance cash value	
	S
	S
	S
	S
Subtotal	S

Other Assets (house, vehicles)	Use Zillow.com to get an estimate of the value of your house and Kelley Blue Book for an estimate of the value of your vehicles.
	S
	S
	S
	S
Subtotal	S

TOTAL ASSETS

Liabilities (the stuff I owe)

Real estate mortgage/equity loans

	S
	S
	S
	S
Subtotal	S

Vehicle loans

	S
	S
	S
	S
Subtotal	S

Student loans

	S
	S
	S
Subtotal	S

Personal loans

	S
	S
	S
Subtotal	S

Credit card and other consumer debt

Only include balances that you carry forward from month to month. If you pay off your balance every month, it's not debt!

	S
	S
	S
	S
	S
	S
Subtotal	S

TOTAL LIABILITIES

TOTAL ASSETS [ ] — TOTAL LIABILITIES [ ]

Subtract your liabilities from your assets to get net worth. = **NET WORTH** [ ]

Congratulations!

Wow! Congratulations! Calculating your net worth, your starting point, is a significant achievement. Can I let you in on a little secret? Make it a tradition to record your net worth every January 1st. You'll be amazed by how it grows year after year.

I understand that removing judgment and emotion from your net worth calculation can be challenging. Here are some things to keep in mind.

☑ If you're young and grappling with student loan debt (and maybe a mortgage), it's possible that your net worth is in the red. But fret not, this is entirely normal. You'll shift into the positive as you conquer debt and amass assets.

☑ The value of your investments can sway with the broader economy. But here's the silver lining: even during market slumps, you can bolster your net worth by paying down debt.

☑ Challenge yourself to boost your net worth annually. Aim for a specific growth target, whether it's $10,000, $100,000, or 10% higher than the previous year. Make a commitment, take actionable steps, and proudly document your progress!

This is how I feel about my net worth: (circle one)

☹ ☹ 😐 🙂 😊

My Thoughts about my Net Worth

Create Mile Markers

Imagine your first task on this exciting road trip is to get out of town. I'll provide you with mile markers and directions to guide you onto those wide highways. From there, it's up to you to decide whether to take the expressway or opt for the scenic route.

One thing that often holds people back from embarking on this journey is the number of options. When should you start? Where should you head to? Who should you bring along? What's your budget? It can all feel quite overwhelming at times.

But here's the parallel to our financial freedom journey. You've already got a solid grasp of how much you need, what you currently have, and the lifestyle you aspire to. So, picture yourself in the driver's seat, trusting your financial GPS to guide you towards financial freedom. The first step? Let's hit the road and get you out of town!

Mile Marker 1:
Save at least $1,000 in an emergency fund

You're all revved up, ready to hit the road on this exciting journey. You turn the key, shift into drive, and suddenly, KAPOW! A flat tire! A quick check reveals your tires are in terrible shape and won't last the trip. It's time to head to the tire shop, and yes, it comes with an unexpected expense.

It's almost a given that unexpected things will crop up. Just when you're feeling confident about the road ahead, life throws a curveball. To stay on track without diving into debt, you need to have $1,000 in cash ready. Don't let these surprises throw you off course. Set up a separate emergency fund, or keep the cash tucked away securely. If possible, aim for $2,000, just in case. I want you to get those new tires so you can pick up your friends and keep this road trip rolling! Use the fun race form at the end of this chapter to record your progress.

☐ Yes, I have $1,000 in my emergency fund.

My emergency fund balance: _____

Mile Marker 2:
Get the full employer retirement match

Im thrilled you have those new tires! Now, picture this: Your boss has a fantastic surprise in store for you. She knows how dedicated you are, so she's willing to match you gallon for gallon (or amp for amp) for the fuel you use on this trip. How incredible is that? Let's say you spend $50 to fill up the car, and your boss will cover the next $50 of your fuel expenses. Amazing, right?

Of course, you wouldn't pass up that free money! Well, the same principle applies to your retirement fund. Most employers offer a matching program, and it's essentially free money for your future. Never turn down free money! Every employer has its unique matching rules (check with Human Resources if you're unsure). Set up automatic contributions from your paycheck and cash in on that fantastic benefit!

☐ Yes, I contribute to my retirement fund and receive matching funds.

My retirement contributions: _____ per paycheck

3 Mile Marker 3
Pay off high-interest debt

Now, let's confront another common roadblock that can put a significant dent in your journey to financial freedom - high-interest debt. Picture yourself on a road trip, towing a heavy anchor tied to your bumper; that's the burden of high-interest debt. Whether it's credit card balances, personal loans, or other financial obligations with high interest rates, these financial anchors can significantly slow down your progress. It's high time to cut them loose.

So, what exactly constitutes high-interest debt? While interest rates can fluctuate and depend on the type of loan, we'll use 8 percent as our threshold. If the interest rate on a particular debt surpasses this mark, put it on your priority list. In most cases, if you're carrying credit card debt, it's likely your biggest anchor weighing you down. Let's free ourselves from that anchor!

☐ Yes, I paid off all of my high-interest debt

4 Mile Marker 4:
Save 6 months worth of expenses

This is a cross-country road trip, my friend. Anything can happen. Let's say the road ahead is blocked by an unexpected detour. What do you do? You have the peace of mind knowing that you have enough fuel in the tank to take an alternate route. Similarly, in your financial journey, build enough savings to cover at least six months' worth of living expenses. Consider it your financial detour insurance!

Why six months? Well, it offers a comfortable cushion to cover expenses if life throws you a curveball, like a job loss, medical emergency, or unexpected home repair. It means you won't be forced to rely on high-interest debt or dip into your long-term investments. It's your ticket to smoother sailing on your financial journey. And hey, it gets you that much closer to reaching the financial security mark!

☐ Yes, I have enough in savings to cover 6 months worth of expenses
My savings fund balance: _____

GREAT JOB!

Hooray! You're on a roll, making remarkable strides on your financial journey. As you venture beyond the city limits, it's up to you to chart your course. Your decisions are guided by your values, knowledge, and aspirations. There's no definitive path; every mile marker is a step closer to your destination.

Number your Mile Markers

You've successfully passed mile markers one through four with flying colors. Now, let's shift our focus to the next phase of your journey towards financial freedom. The road ahead presents six more mile markers, and you have the privilege of choosing their order. Take a moment to reflect on your priorities and arrange these markers (5 through 10) in your preferred sequence. Simply write the corresponding number inside each mile marker icon. For example, trimming your expenses might be your preferred next move, so you would put the number '5' in the circle. Add comments in the notes.

Max out retirement contributions

Notes

Trim my expenses

Notes

Supercharge my savings

Notes

Destroy my debt

Notes

Build a diversified investment portfolio

Notes

Notes

Increase my income

Here's the inside scoop on your mile marker exercise. While it would be great if we could tackle all the mile marker activities simultaneously, there's something called 'decision paralysis.' It's when we're faced with so many decisions that we end up choosing no action as the easiest path, leaving us stuck at mile marker zero! And that's why you assigned priority levels to your mile markers, providing you with a clear and manageable route forward. No more decision overload!

Now that you've set your priorities, let's talk about speed. How fast do you want to reach your destination? Are you eager to zip down the freeway, aiming for a swift arrival? Or perhaps you're enticed by the scenic route, with its charming detours to quirky attractions? Maybe you're even open to a mix of both! The road ahead is wide open! Tell me, what's your driving style?

○	○	○
Freeway all the way!	Scenic route, please!	Maybe a bit of both?

The routes you choose on this financial road trip are influenced by your personal values, your unique circumstances, and, to some extent, sheer luck. While it's tempting to believe that your journey to financial freedom is solely a test of your skills and endurance, unexpected challenges like wildfires and mechanical problems, can disrupt your trip. It's a reality we all face.

Here's a piece of advice: seize the opportunities when they come your way. Life has its ups and downs, like the ebb and flow of a journey. There will be times when everything seems to align perfectly – your investments are thriving, your career is on fire, your expenses are trimmed down, and your health is robust. It's like a sunny day on the open road.

But then, you hit a roadblock. You might face unexpected challenges like a job loss or mounting medical bills. When you find yourself on the expressway to success during those good times, make the most of it. Move as quickly as you can towards your financial goals. This way, you'll have the flexibility to slow down and enjoy the scenic route or navigate detours when life takes an unexpected turn.

> "All you need is the plan, the road map, and the courage to press on to your destination."
>
> **- Earl Nightingale**

Your journey is entirely your own, so there's no need to compare it to someone else's adventure. Be true to yourself! If something doesn't align with your instincts or if an exceptional opportunity arises, don't let your plan dictate your choices. Of course, gather information, weigh the pros and cons, but ultimately, let your heart guide your decision-making. Let's explore a couple of examples.

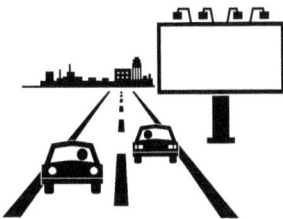

Ryan and Kai Take the Fast Lane

Meet Ryan and Kai, a dynamic couple who are determined to reach financial freedom as fast as possible. They've already tackled the first four mile markers, and now they're ready to sprint down the financial freeway. Their top priority is to max out retirement contributions. They've calculated that by aggressively contributing to their retirement accounts, they can take advantage of compound interest and turbocharge their investments. They both allocate a significant portion of their income toward their 401(k) and IRA accounts, ensuring they meet the annual contribution limits.

Next up, they decide to grow their income. Kai takes on freelance consulting work in his spare time, while Ryan explores opportunities for career advancement. This boost in income not only accelerates their journey but also provides a safety net for unexpected expenses.

To further optimize their path, they've chosen to supercharge their savings. They trimmed their expenses and automated transfers to a high-yield savings account. They will soon reach their initial goal - financial security. They are also careful to build a diversified investment portfolio.

Lastly, they commit to destroying debt. They prioritize paying off their student loans and car loans to reduce their financial liabilities. As a result of their laser-focused approach on the freeway to financial freedom, Kai and Ryan steadily make progress toward their goal, and they have a significant cushion to handle road emergencies.

Michelle's Scenic Route

Meet Michelle, a single mom with a demanding professional job and the sole responsibility of caring for her young daughter, Lily. Michelle is determined to provide a secure future for Lily while taking the scenic route to financial freedom.

Michelle's top priority is ensuring Lily's well-being, so she prioritizes growing her income. She leverages her professional skills to negotiate a raise at work. Moreover, she's actively investing in her own personal development by diligently working towards completing a certification program, which will open doors to higher positions on her career ladder.

Michelle is focused on supercharging her savings. She diligently saves a portion of her income each month, contributing to her savings, dream, and retirement accounts. By automating her savings, she ensures consistent progress toward her financial goals. Michelle understands the importance of trimming expenses without compromising her family's quality of life. She carefully evaluates their monthly spending and finds ways to reduce costs without sacrificing their needs or experiences.

Once her savings goals are met, Michelle goes on a mission to destroy debt. Her extra income from her promotion goes directly toward paying off her student and car loans. Michelle's personality leans toward Scout - she has a tendency to play it safe. So she is slowly dipping her toe into investing, starting small and investing in low-cost index funds.

While Michelle's journey may not be as rapid as others on the freeway, she embraces the scenic route. She enjoys quality time with Lily, explores budget-friendly family activities, and appreciates the journey's unique experiences.

Your initial position in this race, such as your age and net worth, influences your route. If you're starting out young and with minimal debt, you've got a broader range of choices. You can prioritize loading up your retirement account, knowing that once you hit your target, you can redirect your savings to other purposes, including some well-deserved fun! With plenty of time ahead, your investments have ample opportunity to flourish.

However, if you find yourself starting later in life with substantial debt, jumping on the freeway becomes imperative. You might have noticed that setting up a college fund isn't among the six markers. Take Michelle's story, for instance; there was no mention of a college fund for Lily. While it's a goal Michelle hopes to tackle down the road, she's aware that her current focus on increasing her income, savings, and investments is in her best interest (and Lily's too). The college fund can come later.

Your financial journey isn't limited to just the freeway or the scenic route. Think of it as a highway with multiple exit and entrance ramps along the way. Kai and Ryan might decide to slow down as they approach their goals, savoring the sunsets together. Michelle might consider hopping onto the freeway when Lily is older. The key is flexibility – adapt your route as needed and don't forget to savor the journey called life!

On the next page, you'll discover 10 markers on the road to financial freedom. Transfer your road markers and assign a target end date to each marker..

 START

 **1** Save at least $1,000 in an emergency fund

Date: _____

 **2** Get the full employer retirement match

Date: _____

 Write down your goals and a target completion date

 **3** Pay off high-interest debt

Date: _____

 **4** Save 6 months worth of expenses

Date: _____

 **5** Goal:

Date: _____

 **6** Goal:

Date: _____

 **7** Goal:

Date: _____

 **8** Goal:

Date: _____

 **9** Goal:

Date: _____

 **10** Goal:

Date: _____

 FINISH

Savings Goal

$1,000

$1,000

$900

$800

$700

$600

$500

$400

$300

$200

$100

$0

START

You Got This!

Notes:

AWESOME!

Happy dance! Here's hoping you're still grooving to your playlist. Be proud of yourself – you've covered a lot of ground, and your money game is on fire!

☐ You know how much money you need to reach financial security, freedom, and independence.

You were bold, scrutinizing your purchases through the lens of wants and needs. What revelations did you unearth? Perhaps you realized your spending didn't quite match your priorities, or maybe you found yourself right on track. The beauty is, you now have a foundation to gauge your desired financial level, whether it's for a frugal, comfortable, or luxurious lifestyle. Don't let the number hold you back; we'll delve into the "HOW" in the next chapter!

☐ You calculated your net worth - you know your starting point.

Oh, that net worth number never deceives. It's our 'North Star,' the unwavering measure of our wealth. You've done a stellar job documenting your assets and liabilities, revealing your net worth. And the secret to elevating it? Boost your assets, diminish those liabilities. It truly is that straightforward. Keep in mind, your net worth is just a number; it doesn't define you. Chart your annual progress, take a step back, and marvel at your remarkable achievements.

☐ You set up mile markers and stated your preferred route.

The path to financial freedom might seem complex, but not when you have mile markers. You've already covered the initial four markers to kickstart your journey, and you've ranked the importance of six more markers to steer you forward. You even have an idea of whether you prefer the freeway, the scenic route, or a mix of both. Your roadmap is ready, and you've worked some financial magic in this chapter! So go ahead, celebrate with your favorite song, dance a little, and give yourself a well-deserved pat on the back. Great work!

Notes

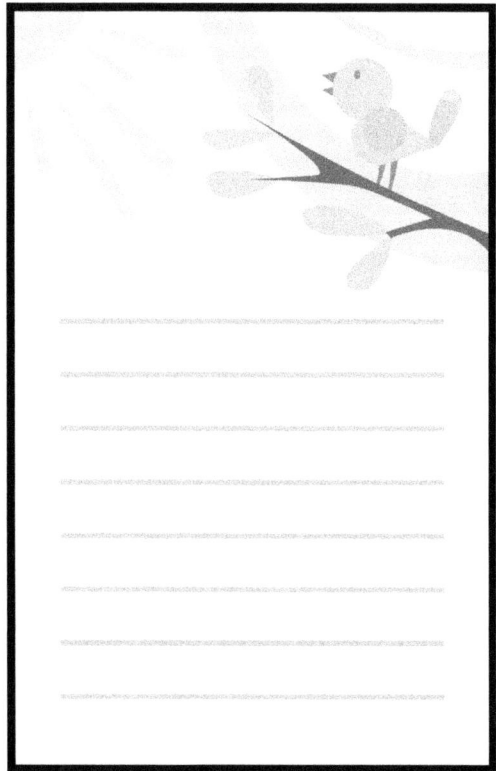

5

FIRE UP YOUR ENGINE!

Fire up your Engine

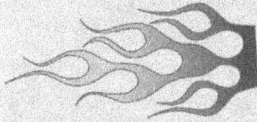

You've got your map, and you're all set to roll! Let's hit the road and rev up that financial engine. We'll do it by boosting your income, trimming expenses, and stashing away the surplus. Are you ready to ignite your financial journey?

Objectives

- To understand the basics of the FIRE movement.
- To estimate the number of years to financial freedom
- To create a plan that widens the gap between income and expenses

Big Mission

Our mission is to introduce you to the FIRE movement and equip you with income-producing and expense-cutting strategies that will propel you towards financial freedom.

To-do Checklist

- ☐ Estimate the number of years to financial freedom
- ☐ Strategize ways to grow your income
- ☐ Trim your expenses
- ☐ Put your plan together

Get Excited about FIRE

Buckle up, because we're about to take a trip back to the late 1980s. Yep, we're slipping back into the era of big hair, boomboxes, and a book that would change the way people thought about money forever. We're talking about "Your Money or Your Life" by Vicki Robin and Joe Dominguez. This book was like a financial compass, pointing people toward a path they never thought possible - early retirement!

Fast forward to today, and that spark from the late '80s has turned into a blazing movement known as FIRE (Financial Independence, Retire Early). It's a community of people who have taken the lessons from "Your Money or Your Life" and run with them. But here's the twist. The modern movement is less about early retirement and more about financial independence (FI).

In my perspective, I like to believe that FIRE is short for Financial Independence, Rediscover and Explore. Why? Because once you've got your financial house in order and can break free from the traditional workforce, you've unlocked the opportunity to rediscover your true self and explore your deepest desires. Get ready to embark on this transformative journey of financial empowerment!

The Most Exciting Grid you'll Ever See

I can talk about FIRE all day long, but it's more powerful if I SHOW you! On the next page, you'll find a MAGIC GRID (created by Zach at Four Pillar Freedom). It will show you how long it will take you to reach financial independence. Mind you, this is the ultimate point where work becomes optional (stick around for our experiment on financial freedom). Here are the assumptions on which the graph is based.

Your Starting Net Worth = $0

Average Annual Rate of Return = 5%

Financial Independence = 25 x annual expenses

If you'd like to tinker with these assumptions, visit Zach's Four Pillar Freedom webpage –

bit.ly/FIREgrid

Annual Spending

	S40k	S60k	S80k	S100k	S120k	S140k	S160k	S180k	S200k
S180k									51.4
S160k								49.1	36.7
S140k							46.7	34.5	28.0
S120k						43.9	31.9	25.7	21.6
S100k					40.6	29.0	23.1	19.3	16.6
S80k				36.7	25.7	20.1	16.6	14.2	12.4
S60k			31.9	21.6	16.6	13.6	11.5	10.0	8.8
S40k		25.7	16.6	12.4	10.0	8.3	7.1	6.3	5.6
S20k	16.6	10.0	7.1	5.6	4.6	3.9	3.4	3.0	2.7

After-Tax Annual Income

Let's break down this grid. Start with your annual after-tax income on the bottom row (gross income minus taxes). Then, find the row that most closely matches your annual spending, which we've organized in S20,000 increments. It won't be a perfect match, but it'll get you in the ballpark. Now, pay attention to the squares with light shading; those indicate results that can lead you to financial independence in 10 years or less. The squares with dark shading represent a path to financial independence in 20 years or less. Let's explore a few examples to make it even clearer.

★ ★ ★ ★ ★ Xue and Chris bring in S180,000 in after-tax annual income. Their annual spending is S100,000. They will reach financial independence in 19.3 years.

★ ★ ★ Heather has an annual after-tax income of S80,000. Her expenses are S60,000. She can reach financial independence in 31.9 years.

★ Dave makes S200,000 in annual after-tax income. He spends S200,000 each year. Dave will NEVER reach financial independence. If he cuts his expenses to S180,000 (he's saving 10%) he can reach financial independence in 51.4 years.

80

Now, brace yourself for the thrilling part! Take a good look at the grid below. There's one exciting twist here - we're no longer aiming for financial independence (25 times annual expenses); we're gunning for financial freedom! In this grid, our target is 10 times annual expenses, and hitting this milestone opens the door to part-time work, adventurous new business ventures, sabbaticals for fun and exploration, or whatever audacious scheme your creative mind conjures up. Ready to dive in?

Years to Financial Freedom (10 x annual expenses)

Annual Spending	$40k	$60k	$80k	$100k	$120k	$140k	$160k	$180k	$200k
$180k									34.9
$160k								33.0	22.5
$140k							30.8	20.7	15.8
$120k						28.4	18.8	14.2	11.5
$100k					25.7	16.6	12.4	10.0	8.3
$80k				22.5	14.2	10.5	8.3	6.9	5.9
$60k			18.8	11.5	8.3	6.5	5.4	4.6	4.0
$40k		14.2	8.3	5.9	4.6	3.7	3.2	2.7	2.4
$20k	8.3	4.6	3.2	2.4	2.0	1.6	1.4	1.2	1.1

After-Tax Annual Income

Let's circle back to our savvy financial adventurers, Xue and Chris, along with Heather, and peek under the hood at their strategy-shifting plans. Sadly, Dave's sitting this trip out; seems he's still a bit too attached to his spending habits. But that's okay, not everyone's ready to ride shotgun on the road to financial freedom.

"Life is a journey, not a destination."
- Ralph Waldo Emerson

Xue and Chris' Countdown to Cribs

Xue and Chris are our dynamic duo with a firm grip on their finances, reeling in a hefty $180,000 after taxes while only spending a cool $80,000. They hit a speed bump in their financial journey, feeling the pinch of a 19-year wait to their independence day. But then, they caught a glimpse of the financial freedom grid, and their world turned technicolor. They crunched the numbers and—boom!—realized they could reach their 10x expenses goal in less than 7 years. Talk about flipping the script!

The dream of adding tiny sneakers to their shoe rack had always been there, but they'd shelved it amidst their bustling careers and the dollar signs attached to child-rearing. Now, they're letting themselves wade back into those parenthood waters. Xue, with her tech-savvy brain wired for AI, is revving up for a home-based side hustle that could balance the books and still leave room for lullabies. The plan? To dial down her 9-to-5 as she dials up her consultancy, paving a way to flex around future family time.

The financial forecast is looking bright, and they're buzzing with anticipation. Diapers, daycare, and the whole nine yards seem less like a financial juggle and more like the exciting next chapter.

Heather's Vintage Clothing Passport

Heather had every reason to be proud, stashing away a cool $20,000 from her $80,000 after-tax income annually. But when she learned that this savings tempo meant a 32-year tango in the corporate world—her spirits dipped. It was like staring down a long, straight highway with no rest stops in sight. Then came a game-changer: the financial freedom grid. This wasn't just a chart; it was a revelation, showing her that at this rate, she could cut the cord on her office badge in under 19 years. Better, but still an eternity in office years.

That's when the light bulb flickered on over Heather. She realized this grid was more than a timetable; it was a launchpad for big ideas. It got her gears turning—why wait for financial freedom at a snail's pace? She started envisioning a life where her money worked for her, not the other way around. That's when her online store idea took shape. Buy sought-after vintage clothing from garage sales and flea markets and resell them in her curated online shop. Bonus! She partnered with her sister, who managed and shipped the inventory.

Heather's online store wasn't just about business; it was her ticket to globetrotting without a return date. Every sale was a step closer to her year-long travel dream, exchanging spreadsheets for backpacks and team meetings for world explorations. It was a bold move, a way to shift from the slow lane to the express route to freedom. And with her strategy unfolding, Heather was charting a course for a future where her passport got more use than her printer.

⚠ **HAZARD: Avoid the trap of having your wealth tied up in your home while lacking accessible funds.**

When you took a moment to tally up your net worth, what did it reveal? For many in the U.S., their home emerges as their greatest asset, shadowed closely by their mortgage as their largest liability. The big question is, how can you tap into the value of your home? Options include drawing from a home equity loan—adding to your debts—or putting up a 'For Sale' sign. Either choice leads to the same dilemma: You still need a place to kick back, be it a four-bedroom or the cozy confines of an RV.

As you cruise through this chapter, let's explore smart paths to passive income that won't monopolize your time—imagine earning from rental properties or collecting royalties from your bestselling book. Consider the extra dough you could rake in from a side hustle. This is the time to steer your hard-earned income into tax-advantaged accounts, like your retirement nest egg, as well as into taxable investment accounts.

The goal? Financial liberation without being compelled to hand over your house keys, unless that's part of your grand plan. It's about crafting financial freedom that meshes seamlessly with the life you aspire to lead.

MOVE FORWARD GOOD Things ARE UP AHEAD

Grow the Gap

Securing your financial future hinges on a simple yet powerful concept: expanding the margin between your income and expenses. The formula is straightforward—the greater your income and the smaller your expenses, the more golden opportunities you create for yourself. This is the secret sauce, the alchemist's stone that can transform your financial outlook. Embrace the art of saving and the wisdom of investing that surplus, and watch as it paves the way to an extraordinary tomorrow.

Turn the page, and you're in for a treat—a graphic that's your roadmap to a financial adventure! We're zooming in on two crucial signposts: Income and Expenses. Ready to dive in? You might want to queue up that epic playlist from the last chapter – it's going to be quite the ride!

My Path to Financial Freedom

Annual Income

After-tax Pay

Side hustles, windfalls, passive income

GROW THE GAP!
Income - Expenses

Annual Expenses

Housing

Food

Transportation

Other

After-tax Pay

_____

Annual Income

Side hustles, windfalls,
passive income

_____

TOTAL INCOME _____

Let's unpack the 'income growth' segment of the wealth-building equation. A mix-and-match of income streams is fantastic, but let's keep it real—not everyone's lifestyle or schedule can stretch to fit a side gig, especially if you're clocking in serious hours at a well-paying job and already playing the balancing act with family life. And that's okay! Often, a little financial fine-tuning and a commitment to your long-term goals can reveal that your current paycheck is more than capable of fueling your trip to financial freedom.

Grab a pen and let's bask in the glow of your income as we lay it out on paper. Start with your annual net salary, the star of the show, and then spotlight any additional acts like side hustle earnings, unexpected windfalls—think bonuses, inheritances, tax refunds—and any passive income streams. This is the cast of characters that makes up your financial play!

> Passive income is money you earn that doesn't require active work to continue generating. For example, royalties from a book, dividends from a stock investment, or rental income. Each source required some upfront investment in time or money, but now the money flows in without a lot of work.

There's a whole spectrum of choices waiting for you when it comes to boosting your income. Cast your eyes over the list below and tick off the options that spark your interest. Whether it's asking for a raise, starting a side hustle, or investing for passive income, there's a wealth of routes you can explore. Find the ones that resonate with your skills and lifestyle, and you could see your financial picture start to bloom.

- [ ] Negotiate a raise or promotion with a higher salary

- [ ] Switch companies for a better income or opportunities

- [ ] Complete a program of study that will qualify you for a higher salary

- [ ] Start freelancing or consulting in your spare time

- [ ] Find a side hustle that brings in extra income

- [ ] Invest in real estate

- [ ] Invest in high-dividend yielding stocks

- [ ] Other _____

Thoughts and Ideas

GO Negotiate your Salary

Boosting your income often involves negotiating a raise or securing a strong initial salary. While it can seem daunting, here are some straightforward tips to help you through the process.

☐ Find out what others are earning

- Co-workers with similar education, experience, and responsibilities
- Similar positions in competitor organizations
- National and regional salaries for your occupation

☐ Figure out a reasonable salary request - seek specific salary (not a range)

- Consider your education, credentials, experience, and level of responsibilities
- Take location into account – jobs in large cities usually pay more

☐ Gauge your employer's health - can they afford to give out raises?

- Is your company on a hiring spree? Are they freezing open positions?
- What does the latest financial report look like?

☐ List the reasons you deserve a raise

- What are your accomplishments? Be specific and focus on your most recent
- How have your responsibilities changed over time?
- What are your relevant skills – include hard skills, like technical writing, and soft skills, like collaborating with partners.
- What will you do for the organization in the future? What are your long-term goals?

☐ Consider your timing

- Request raise after a big accomplishment
- Request raise well in advance of your performance review (budgets are often set before reviews).
- Try asking when there's a new fiscal year, there's new funding, or the finances of the organization look promising.

☐ Set up an appointment and consider your alternatives

- Schedule an appointment, preferably for a morning (avoid mid- to late-afternoons)
- Decide in advance what you will do if your boss says "no"
- Are you willing to quit?
- Will you ask again at a later date?

☐ **Present your case**
- Give yourself a pep talk before you enter the office
- Stick to the facts. Stay calm. Do NOT talk about personal troubles or your expenses.
- Focus on how you will help the organization grow

☐ **Present your case**
- Give yourself a pep talk before you enter the office
- Stick to the facts. Stay calm. Do NOT talk about personal troubles or your expenses.
- Focus on how you will help the organization grow

☐ **Get the raise . . . or not!**
- If you get a raise, ask about timing – are there next steps and when will the raise go into effect. And celebrate!
- Have a back-up plan if the answer is "no"
  - Get feedback on what you need to do to qualify for a raise. Come up with a plan for what you need to do to get a raise by your next performance review.
  - If you feel like the raise conversation was a dead-end and you are not valued at your current organization, start looking around for other opportunities.

"If you don't ask, the answer is always no"
- Nora Roberts

Get a Side Hustle

GO

If your paycheck isn't cutting it for financial freedom, or if entrepreneurship beckons, consider starting a side hustle!

Let's do a quick check-in. How interested are you in side hustles?

O   O   O
Not interested   Interested   Super interested

Building a profitable side hustle requires some research and a dash of experimentation. Before fully committing, it's a smart move to "test drive" different side hustles to find the one that suits you best. If you're wondering where to start, two fantastic resources, Side Hustle Nation and Side Hustle School, offer valuable guidance to help you navigate the intricacies of side hustling.

sidehustlenation.com

sidehustleschool.com

Once you find a side hustle that sounds good to you, ask yourself these questions:

Why does this side hustle appeals to me?

What skills can I bring to this side hustle?

My friends say that this side hustle, given my skills and personality, would be a:

O   O   O   O

Lousy fit   So-so fit   Pretty good fit   Great fit!

I'm genuinely proud of your progress! Boosting your income can be a bit challenging, but you've handled it like a pro. As we conclude this leg of our journey, take a moment to jot down your current income and your desired income.

Type of Income	Current annual income	Desired annual income	Difference
Salary / Paychecks			
Side hustles			
Windfalls			
Passive Income			
TOTAL			

It's time to reveal your game plan for reaching that coveted ideal income level. Will it involve pursuing a raise or promotion, exploring new job opportunities, starting a side hustle, exploring passive income streams, or something else entirely? Write down your #1 winning idea below.

My #1 super idea for boosting my income:

Trim your Expenses

Annual Expenses

Housing	Transportation	Food	Other
_____	_____	_____	_____

TOTAL EXPENSES _____

Let's shift our focus to the other side of the financial freedom equation - expenses. You've done an excellent job categorizing your wants and needs and have a clear picture of your expense levels for a frugal, comfortable, and luxurious lifestyle. It's now time to delve into strategies for reducing those expenses. While there are various ways to trim your spending, such as sacrificing your daily latte or canceling unused subscriptions, the most significant impact can be achieved by addressing the "Big Three" - housing, transportation, and food.

Enter your annual expenses in the boxes above. If you have significant expenses under the "Other" category, such as health insurance premiums or childcare costs, you can note those separately. Calculate your total annual expenses, and if estimating makes it simpler, go ahead and make your best guess.

Minimalism will Accelerate your Journey

If you're eager to fast-track your journey to financial freedom, think of minimalism as your secret turbo boost. Plus, it's like giving the planet a high-five because minimalism is eco-friendly – you're making a smaller Earthly impact. So, what's minimalism all about?

In a world where we're nudged to accumulate more and more "stuff," minimalism is a counter-culture. You'll be driving against traffic, and you'll feel great about it! Minimalism is all about simplifying your life, cutting through the clutter, and focusing on what truly matters – whether it's in your physical space or your finances.

When you bring minimalism into your financial game, it's like giving your spending habits a mindfulness makeover. Instead of mindlessly splurging, minimalists carefully ponder each purchase, asking themselves, "Does this align with my values? Does it spark joy or serve a real purpose?" This change in mindset can lead to fewer impulsive buys and a more thoughtful use of your resources.

Minimalism also extends its magic to decluttering your financial world. Think streamlined accounts, automated bill payments, and neatly organized financial documents. All of this simplification means less stress, more time saved, and a smoother ride on your journey toward financial freedom. It's like having your financial affairs on cruise control, leaving you with more time and energy to enjoy the ride.

Here's how I feel about minimalism for my lifestyle (circle one).

Your financial decisions should align with your values, and in today's world, there's a pressing issue called climate change that demands our attention. Every spending choice you make can affect the planet. Look for ways to reduce expenses while also making environmentally conscious decisions. This might mean that you make a higher upfront investment in products or practices that will ultimately save you money over time. The planet will THANK YOU!

The "Big 3" Expenses: Housing

Alright, let's dive into the topic of housing, one of the biggest expenses for most people. Before we get into the nitty-gritty, here's a little heads-up: the housing market is like a rollercoaster, always up and down. While owning a home might seem like the ultimate American dream, it's not necessarily the smartest choice at all times, especially when interest rates are sky-high, and home values are through the roof!

Time to put those housing expenses on paper. Write down your current monthly housing costs and then multiply that by 12 to get your yearly expenditure. Now, here's the fun part - take a close look at each of those expenses and ask yourself the magical question: "Can I lower my costs?" Go ahead and circle that answer, aiming for a resounding YES!

	Monthly Expenses	Yearly Expenses (x 12)	Can I lower my costs?
Rent or Mortgage			Yes / No / NA
Renters / Homeowners Insurance			Yes / No / NA
HOA Fees			Yes / No / NA
Utilities (electric, gas, water)			Yes / No / NA
Property taxes			Yes / No / NA
Maintenance or repairs			Yes / No / NA
TOTAL			

REMEMBER YOUR WHY

Let's delve into some SUPER MOVES, housing strategies that can significantly slash your housing expenses. These moves may necessitate a shift in lifestyle and some creative thinking, but they can deliver substantial savings. Let's explore three super moves.

1 Downsize or "right size" - lower your square footage (you'll save on mortgage, utilities, and insurance).

2 Become a landlord by buying a duplex or home with an in-law suite that you can rent out. Let your tenants and housemates pay your mortgage!

3 Geoarbitrage - move from a high cost of living area to one with lower costs (domestic or international); ideal for remote workers.

SUPER MOVES are definitely worth considering, but they may not be possible or practical at this point in your life. No problem! There are plenty of other ways you can reduce your housing costs. Place a checkmark next to each strategy you can try.

Shop around for a better insurance policy (bundle home and auto for a better rate).

Close off rooms that aren't used to save energy; get a programmable thermostat.

Refinance if it makes sense. Consider moving from a 30-year loan to a 15-year loan to save on interest payments.

Request a property tax reassessment if there are discrepancies in the assessment report.

Cut down on landscaping and water expenses by using native low-maintenance plants.

Go solar. You'll have upfront costs (look for local and national incentive programs), but you'll save on your utility bills.

The "Big 3" Expenses: Transportation

Transportation is one of the "Big 3" expenses, and it's deeply intertwined with the American way of life. The modern cityscape was shaped by a car-centric culture, with suburbs sprawling around central cities and highways jammed with countless vehicles. In numerous areas, public transportation falls short, making car ownership a practical necessity rather than a luxury.

Just as you tackled the housing expenses table like a pro, it's time to jot down your transportation costs. Record your monthly transportation expenses and then multiply them by 12 to determine your annual spending. After that, scrutinize each of these expenses, and aim to find opportunities to say "YES" to reducing your costs.

	Monthly Expenses	Yearly Expenses (x 12)	Can I lower my costs?
Public transportation & rideshares			Yes / No / NA
Fuel (gasoline, electric charges)			Yes / No / NA
Parking and tolls			Yes / No / NA
Vehicle maintenance			Yes / No / NA
Auto insurance			Yes / No / NA
Maintenance or repairs			Yes / No / NA
Auto loan(s)			Yes / No / NA
Registration / emissions fees			Yes / No / NA
Other transportation costs			Yes / No / NA
TOTAL			

You have the opportunity to make some SUPER MOVES that can significantly reduce your transportation costs. While these moves may not be feasible for everyone, it's essential to keep an open mind. Let's explore three moves that can have a substantial impact on cutting your transportation expenses.

1 Get rid of a vehicle, especially if you have "extra" vehicles that are seldom used. Or turn your "extra" car into a rental. Combine with remote work for extra savings.

2 Swap out your gas-guzzler for a pre-owned, energy-efficient vehicle. Make the leap to an electric or hybrid car (or even an e-bike).

3 If you live near town, walk or bike to run most of your errands. Take public transportation other days. Rent a car for the occasional outing.

Certainly, there are plenty of other tactics you can employ to reduce your transportation costs. Explore these options below and check each one you're willing to try.

Shop around for a better vehicle insurance policy (bundle).

Don't use premium gasoline (unless the car manufacturer requires it).

Carpool with co-workers or others with the same commute.

Plan your errands so you can efficiently do them in one trip.

Check with your employer to see if they have any discounts for public transportation.

Find a WAY NOT AN EXCUSE

The "Big 3" Expenses: Food

Now, let's talk about another significant expense: food. While inflation can certainly impact our ability to manage food costs and overall expenses, our choices and habits hold even more sway over our budget. Food expenses can pile up rapidly, particularly when we're not keeping a close eye on our spending and indulging in occasional "treats" without thought.

You're nailing this routine! Document your food expenses for the month, then multiply by 12 to determine your annual total. We've kept it simple with just four categories: groceries, dining out, meal services, and alcoholic beverages. Why alcohol? Well, for some folks, it can take a substantial chunk out of their budget. By laying out these numbers, you'll gain a clearer picture of where you can make cuts in your expenses.

	Monthly Expenses	Yearly Expenses (x 12)	Can I lower my costs?
Groceries			Yes / No / NA
Dining out			Yes / No / NA
Meal services			Yes / No / NA
Alcoholic beverages			Yes / No / NA
TOTAL			

Let's dive into some SUPER MOVES that can significantly impact your grocery bills. For many, one particular move can be a game-changer: reducing those frequent restaurant meals. Here are your food strategies to consider.

1 Set reasonable limits on the frequency of dining out. When you do dine out, make these occasions truly memorable.

2 Get cooking! Start by heading to the grocery store with a well-planned list of ingredients for delicious recipes. Be mindful not to over-purchase and end up wasting food.

3 Cut back on alcoholic beverages, reserving them for special celebratory occasions. Or eliminate alcohol altogether!

Other Expenses

Now, let's dive into the "Other" category of expenses. Take a moment to consider the larger expenses in this category or areas where you tend to overspend. Childcare and health insurance are common items here, but you might discover that you're splurging on clothing, gift-giving, antiquing, or any other personal indulgence that's taking a bite out of your budget.

Use the table provided below to input your significant "Other" expenses. Customize it to reflect your specific expenses, and remember to calculate both the monthly and annual costs to get a clear picture of your spending.

	Monthly Expenses	Yearly Expenses (x 12)	Can I lower my costs?
			Yes / No / NA
			Yes / No / NA
			Yes / No / NA
			Yes / No / NA
			Yes / No / NA
			Yes / No / NA
TOTAL			

Write down one or two SUPER MOVES you can make to lower your expenses.

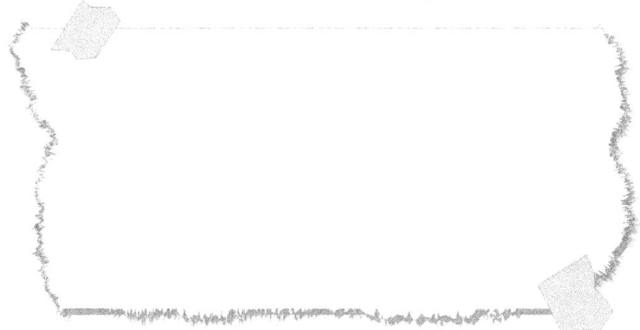

My Desired Expenses

Great job! Awesome progress! Now, use the table below to jot down both your current and desired annual expenses. By calculating the difference, you'll see how much you could potentially save in a year.

Type of Expense	Current annual expense	Desired annual expense	Difference
Housing			
Transportation			
Food			
Other			
TOTAL			

What's your strategy for major savings? Choose the one action that will significantly reduce your yearly expenses. It could be reevaluating your living situation, saying goodbye to a vehicle, or embracing home-cooked meals. Note down your top tactic for financial impact below.

My #1 super idea for trimming my expenses:

Taylor Kicks up her Game

When Taylor first embarked on her career, she adhered to the conventional wisdom of saving 10% of her income. Then she saw our magical grid - that path meant spending the next 51 years chained to her corporate desk, with the distant hope of financial freedom (10 x annual expenses) in 35 years - an eternity!

Taylor's dreams, however, painted a different picture. She envisioned a life where she could work remotely from any corner of the globe. Taylor saw herself powering up her laptop in the morning, then spending the afternoon wandering through vibrant markets, immersing herself in the local culture. This vivid vision ignited a spark within her and served as the driving force to ramp up her savings game.

Taylor wasted no time in accelerating her career. She enthusiastically pursued continuing education and secured certifications that catapulted her into a well-deserved promotion, accompanied by a generous salary boost. It was like merging onto the financial fast lane on her journey to freedom.

But Taylor wasn't content with just a great career; she had a side gig plan. Leveraging her expertise as an AI prompt engineer, she ventured into the gig economy, adding another stream of income and a dose of excitement to her life.

Turning to expenses, Taylor shifted from impulse buying to mindful spending. A reality check came when she tracked her needs and wants, revealing an eye-opening pattern of dining out. She looked back at the blur of mediocre meals she'd consumed in the past month and decided it was time to become the chef of her own adventures. High-quality, nutritious ingredients transformed her dining habits, and as an added bonus, she shed those extra pounds that had been nagging her for years.

With her dual approach of boosting income and slashing expenses, Taylor found herself in a sweet spot. Saving and investing 40% of her income felt effortless, no longer a sacrifice but a well-orchestrated strategy. This put her on a trajectory to achieve financial freedom in less than 12 years. And with her strong skills, she felt comfortable taking a leap if the right opportunity came along.

With a dream and a solid plan, Taylor's journey had transformed from discouragement to electrifying excitement. She eagerly looked forward to the new opportunities that might catapult her into her dream life even sooner. Taylor had gone from feeling stuck to being unstoppable, ready to embrace the thrilling unknown that lay ahead.

Run the Numbers Again

Fantastic work! You're probably recalling that impressive grid from the chapter's start. Let's have some fun with it: plug in your current and desired income and expenses into the Financial Freedom grid (10 x annual expenses). Locate the box that most closely aligns with your figures. For an extra bit of insight, apply the same exercise to the initial grid focused on financial independence (25 x annual expenses). How do your numbers shape up?

	Annual Income	Annual Expenses	Years to Financial Freedom	Years to Financial Indpendence
Current				
Desired				

I hope you're ready to bust a move on this financial journey! Are we in celebration mode yet? If the results aren't quite party-worthy, remember, you've got the roadmap to turn them around. Keep going – you've totally got this!

AWESOME!

Congratulations! You've absolutely nailed it. You're the captain of your destiny, the sovereign of your future, and the maestro of your finances. You've got the foundational knowledge locked down tight. So, let's recap the valuable lessons you've gained in this action-packed chapter.

☐ You estimated how many years to financial independence - and financial freedom - using the powerful MAGIC GRID.

How did you feel when you first looked at the MAGIC GRID? Maybe you were thinking about all that advice you've been given about saving part of your paycheck, and realized it would take decades to get to where you want to go. But then you saw the grid, and realized just how much control you had - manipulating income and expenses - to change your destiny. This is the time to expand your mind and explore different approaches to work and lifestyle.

☐ You researched and strategized ways to grow your income.

Income is one half of the equation. The more income you have, the more you can save! Our ability to increase our income depends on various factors like our skills, market conditions, and the time we can dedicate. What's exciting is that when you develop multiple income streams, if one dries up, you're not stuck along the roadside with a dead battery. You have opportunities waiting. Seize them!

☐ You learned about minimalism and made some big moves to trim your expenses.

If you've been attentive, you've probably noticed that the foundation of our key concepts—financial security, freedom, and independence—is built upon our annual expenses. Consider the influence you hold in shaping your lifestyle choices and your ability to take eco-friendly actions that not only save you money but also contribute to long-term planet preservation. Don't relinquish your power to the consumer-driven society!

Notes

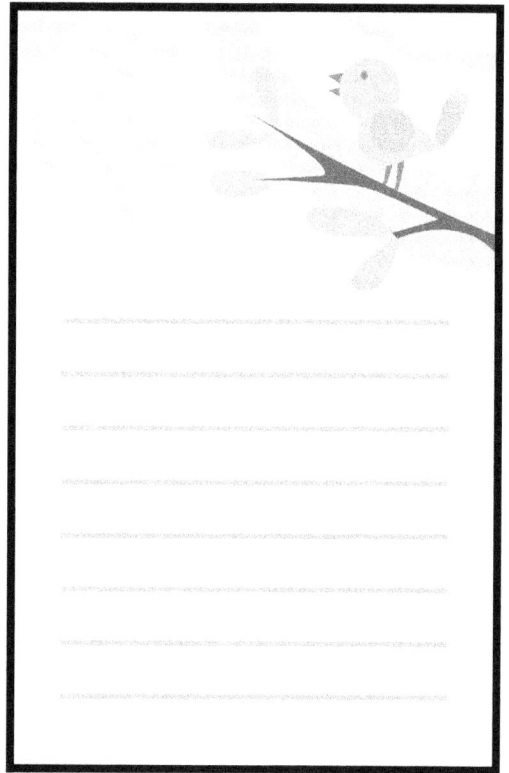

6

RACE THROUGH DEBT DETOUR

DETOUR →

Race through Debt Detour

DETOUR →

Imagine you're on the financial highway to freedom, wind in your hair, and open road ahead. But wait, you spot orange cones up ahead—it's a detour. Debt is like that unexpected roadblock on your journey to financial freedom. Our mission: guide you through it swiftly, minimizing the time lost on this diversion.

Objectives

- To explore the emotional aspect of debt
- To develop a strategic plan for debt repayment
- To gain insight into various forms of debt

Big Mission

Our mission is to help you tackle debt so that you can accelerate your journey to financial freedom.

To-do Checklist

☐ Write a 'Dear Debt' letter

☐ Find your Credit Score

☐ Make a debt repayment plan

☐ Build a game plan for student loan and medical debt

Debt Hurts!

Debt! It's nearly inescapable. Dream of a college degree? There's a student loan waiting. Craving a shiny new car? A loan is ready for you. And, of course, there's that ever-present mortgage for your home sweet home. Let's not overlook the debt piled up from unexpected medical bills, the debt that accumulates when holiday generosity takes over, or the debt incurred during those trying months without a steady paycheck. The truth is, we share a love-hate relationship with debt. We adore the possibilities it offers, yet we despise the years, sometimes even decades, spent repaying borrowed money along with interest. For many of us, debt stings.

You've stashed away a solid $1,000 to act as a buffer against new debt creeping in. Plus, you're diligently channeling enough of your income to grab that employer match for your retirement funds. Now, let's tackle high-interest debt with a keen eye on anything at 8% or higher. As you bid farewell to that expensive debt, you'll soon find yourself with a surplus of cash. This newfound wealth is your ticket to building a robust 6-month cushion in savings and investments. And beyond that? Well, my friend, the possibilities are endless!

ONE WAY ➤   There's only one direction on this detour!

If you've tuned into the advice of some popular financial gurus, you might think they've turned criticizing people for their debt into a competitive sport. But here's the reality: you can't rewind time and undo past decisions. Not everyone in debt splurged on luxury items like Rolex watches. Student loan debt, for instance, wasn't a frivolous expense. And for those dealing with medical debt, you're definitely not alone – it's a leading cause of bankruptcy.

The key thing to remember is that no matter the cause of your debt, it's in the rearview mirror. The past is unchangeable. However, your future is an open road waiting to be explored. This detour is a one-way street; you're committed to paying off your debt and relishing the sweet satisfaction that comes with it.

Many of us have spent decades, or even our entire adult lives, shrouded in the shadow of debt. It's time for a fresh perspective. You have the power to avoid new debt, and you possess the bravery to bid farewell to debt for good. On the next page, you'll find a heartfelt "Dear Debt" breakup letter. Then, it's your turn. Go on, show debt the door – it's time to say your final farewell!

Dear Debt,

I've carried you with me for far too long, and it's time for us to part ways. You sneaked into my life like a shadow, promising convenience and instant gratification. Little did I know, you would become a heavy burden that weighed down my spirit and drained my happiness.

Our relationship began innocently enough. I thought I could manage you, that I could keep you in check. But you grew, lurking in the background, until you became an insurmountable obstacle, casting a dark cloud over my life. You made me feel ashamed, guilty, and anxious. I lost sleep over you, constantly worrying about how to keep you at bay.

You see, Debt, you were never really there for me. You promised me the world, but you only brought stress and despair. You made me question my worth, my choices, and my dreams. I felt trapped, suffocated by your presence.

I've decided that I deserve better. I deserve a life free from your chains, where I can breathe, dream, and thrive. I choose to break up with you, to let you go and reclaim my life. It won't be easy, but I'm determined to pay off what I owe and embrace financial freedom.

This is farewell, Debt. I'm taking back control of my life, and I won't let you hold me back any longer. I'm choosing happiness, peace, and a future without you.

Goodbye forever,

Anonymous

goodbye

Dear Debt,

Check your Credit

Before you dive into debt repayment strategies, I've got a quick task for you. Take a moment to jot down your current credit score. Why, you ask? Well, your credit score plays a pivotal role in determining the interest rate you'll secure, and it can be your ticket to unveiling a hidden shortcut for the speediest debt repayment plan. Here's the scoop: the higher your credit score, the sweeter the deal you can snag.

Credit scores can vary depending on the type of credit and the credit reporting agency. For instance, there's a specific credit score used for credit card applications, another for auto loans, and even a different score for mortgage applications. Additionally, there are three major credit reporting agencies, each with its own data and scoring methods.

But here's the good news: You don't have to make your financial journey complicated. Keeping it simple is the way to go. One convenient and reliable source to check your credit score for free is Credit Karma. They provide you with a clear picture of your credit health without any hidden fees. If you're interested in reviewing your credit reports, you can access them annually at AnnualCreditReport.com at no cost (in the USA). This way, you can stay on top of your financial standing without any hassle.

Credit Score
creditkarma.com

Free Credit Reports
AnnualCreditReport.com

Write down your credit score. Then circle your rating in the FICO Credit Score Range.

My Credit Score _____

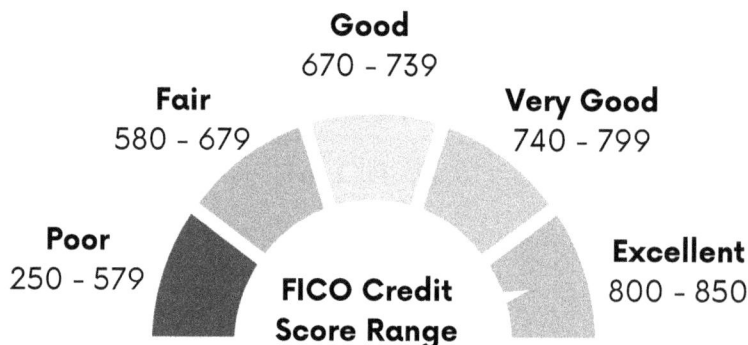

Good
670 - 739

Fair
580 - 679

Very Good
740 - 799

Poor
250 - 579

Excellent
800 - 850

FICO Credit Score Range

Twin Sisters, Different Paths

Meet twin sisters named Bella and Stella. They were inseparable and shared everything, from their childhood toys to their secrets. As they grew older, they both decided it was time to purchase their own homes.

One sunny afternoon, they stumbled upon identical houses, nestled side by side. The houses were exactly what they had been dreaming of, and the amount of the loan each needed was a reasonable $250,000.

Excitedly, Bella and Stella decided to apply for home loans to make their dream of homeownership a reality. However, there was a significant difference between the two sisters when it came to their credit scores.

Bella had always been meticulous about her finances. She had diligently paid her bills on time, kept her credit card balances low, and managed her finances responsibly. As a result, her credit score was an excellent 810. On the other hand, Stella had faced some financial challenges in the past. Her credit score was fair, standing at 600.

When they approached a local bank for mortgage loans, they were quoted different interest rates based on their credit scores. Bella was offered an interest rate of 5.0%, while Stella was offered a higher rate of 7.0%.

Let's do the math to see the impact of these interest rates over the life of their 30-year loans:

Bella's Mortgage
Loan Amount: $250,000
Interest Rate: 5.0%
Monthly Mortgage Payment: $1,342
Total Interest Paid: $482,200

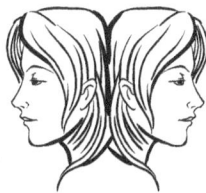

Stella's Mortgage
Loan Amount: $250,000
Interest Rate: 7.0%
Monthly Mortgage Payment: $1,663
Total Interest Paid: $598,800

Over their 30-year loans, Bella will pay approximately $481,200 in interest, while Stella will pay roughly $598,800 - a staggering difference of $117,600!

As they sat together on their newly acquired porches, sipping tea and gazing at their beautiful houses, Bella and Stella realized the profound impact their credit scores had on their financial futures. While both sisters had successfully realized their dreams of homeownership, Bella's outstanding credit score had paved the way for substantial interest savings and lower monthly payments. Stella, spurred by her sister's financial acumen, vowed to make better decisions that will improve her credit score.

How to Raise your Credit Score

Credit scores are not set in stone; they evolve over time. Falling behind on payments can swiftly dent your score, while consistently responsible financial behavior can boost it. As highlighted in the Bella and Stella tale, this seemingly innocuous number wields substantial influence over the cost of your loans and your ability to seize opportunities. Here are four actionable steps to enhance your credit score.

☐ Review credit reports and dispute errors

☐ Pay off cards with a low balance and stop using them

☐ Make payments on time

☐ Lower your credit utilization rate

ⓘ Your **credit utilization rate** is the ratio of your outstanding balance to your credit limit. For example, if your balance is $5,000, and your credit limit is $10,000, your credit utilization rate would be 50%.

To boost your credit score, aim to maintain a credit utilization rate below 30%. Using the example mentioned, you'd need to pay down your balance to $2,900 to achieve a credit utilization rate of 29%. This lower rate can have a positive impact on your credit score.

"The secret of getting ahead is getting started."
- Mark Twain

That's a lot of information! How are you feeling? (circle one).

😟 😕 😐 🙂 😊

Pay off your Debt . . . FAST!

Here we are, navigating this detour together, and it can unfold in one of two ways. We could grumble and watch the clock, dwelling on the time we believe we're squandering. Alternatively, we can view this detour as a challenge and transform our journey to debt freedom into a game. It's a true measure of our dedication to reach our financial destination. I have no doubt you're up for the challenge.

When it comes to paying off debt, there's a multitude of strategies available. While I'm a fan of simplicity, I'm also aware of a hidden path that can help you bypass the slowest segment of this detour. However, this route, my friends, is exclusively accessible if you possess good to excellent credit. So let's begin with the straightforward approach, and then the decision rests with you on whether to accelerate and swiftly maneuver through this detour.

Snowballs and Avalanches

The two most widely recognized strategies are known as the snowball and avalanche methods. Both approaches involve consistently making minimum payments on all your debts, but that's where the similarities end.

Snowball Method	Avalanche Method
Pay off the credit card with the smallest balance as fast as you can.	Pay off the credit card with the highest interest rate first.
Once you've paid off that card, divert extra payments to the card with the next smallest balance.	Once you've paid that off, divert extra payments to the card with the next highest interest rate
Repeat until you're debt-free!	Repeat until you're debt-free!

Whichever strategy you choose, start by gathering your info. You'll find a handy form for credit card debt on the next page, and another for your other debts right after. Priority one: tackle those high-interest credit card debts. Once those are under control, move on to the rest, considering interest rates, terms, and your own priorities. So, before we let the snow settle on our detour, grab your financial info and fill in those forms!

Credit Card Debt

Let's get the ball rolling! Write down the name of your credit card, the current balance owed, the minimum payment amount, the interest rate, and any additional notes. **Use this form exclusively for credit card balances that you do not pay in full each month.**

Description	Balance	Minimum Payment	Interest Rate	Notes

Total Credit Card Debt _____

Which credit card carries the lowest balance?

_____

Which credit card has the highest interest rate?

_____

Other Debt

Use this form to record other types of debt, such as student loans, auto loans, mortgages, medical debt, and personal loans.

Description	Balance	Minimum Payment	Interest Rate	Notes

Total Other Debt _____

Which debt carries the lowest balance?

_____

Which debt has the highest interest rate?

_____

Both methods have their advantages and drawbacks. The snowball method provides a quick sense of achievement as you clear individual credit cards, boosting motivation. However, the avalanche method, which prioritizes interest rates, is financially smarter as it directly targets those costly interest payments. The down side? If you have a high-balance, high-interest card, it might feel like a lengthy journey. The good news is, you can mix and match these strategies to suit your preferences. Start by paying off a low-balance card to get that emotional boost, then shift your focus to the high-interest cards. It's all about finding the approach that works best for you.

Emma and Max Pay off their Debts

Meet two friends, Emma and Max, who had each accumulated $10,000 in credit card debt. Determined to regain control of their finances, they embarked on different journeys to tackle their debt.

Emma was a firm believer in the snowball method. She felt that small victories could lead to big triumphs. Emma began by organizing her credit card debts from the smallest balance to the largest, regardless of interest rates. Her first target was a $1,000 credit card balance. She threw every extra dollar she had at it while continuing to make minimum payments on her other cards. Within a few months, that card was paid off. Emma celebrated this victory with a small treat and then redirected all the money she had been putting towards the first card to the next smallest debt. This snowball effect continued, and Emma gained momentum with each card paid off. Her debt repayment journey felt like a series of small wins, which kept her motivated and energized.

Max, on the other hand, took a different approach. He believed that the avalanche method was the most financially sound strategy. Max prioritized his credit card debts based on their interest rates, from highest to lowest. His highest-interest card had a balance of $2,000. Max allocated as much money as possible to this card while making minimum payments on the others. It took a bit longer to pay off the first card compared to Emma's approach, but Max knew that he was saving money on interest in the long run.

As time passed, Max watched his high-interest debts fall away one by one, leaving only lower-interest cards behind. His progress wasn't as immediately gratifying as Emma's, but he was steadily reducing his overall interest payments.

Fast forward a year, and both Emma and Max had made substantial progress. Emma had paid off five credit cards, with only one remaining. She felt the emotional boost of those small victories along the way and was eager to conquer her last debt. Max, on the other hand, had cleared his high-interest debts efficiently, and his remaining balances were relatively low. He knew that his financial future was looking brighter as he saved money on interest payments.

In the end, Emma and Max had different experiences on their journeys to debt freedom. Emma enjoyed the emotional satisfaction of the snowball method, while Max appreciated the financial benefits of the avalanche approach. The important thing was that they both stuck to their plans, and their determination paid off. They were well on their way to a debt-free future, each having chosen the method that suited their personalities and financial goals best.

Brenda's Blizzard Method

I promised a special route, and it's exclusively for those of you with very good or excellent credit scores. If this describes you, keep reading. If not, head back to the tips on boosting your credit score, and return here when you meet our criteria. For those with an excellent credit score, you're in for the best deals.

☐ Yes, my credit score is Very Good or Excellent

Both the snowball and avalanche strategies are effective, but they can feel like waiting in a construction zone, hoping to be waved through. What if I shared a little-known local road that allows you to bypass the construction zone and rejoin the freeway quickly? It may involve a few extra turns, but in the end, you'll pay the least and achieve debt-free status in the shortest time possible. Think of it as a shortcut to financial freedom.

WARNING
DANGEROUS AREA

The Blizzard Method involves negotiation and scouting for new credit cards featuring low introductory interest rates.

It is **NOT** for you if:

- You are prone to spending and feel tempted to rack up new purchases on the new card.
- You are having difficulty making minimum payments due to a change in circumstances. Instead, call the credit card company and ask for a hardship or repayment plan. Understand the terms before you agree to any offers.

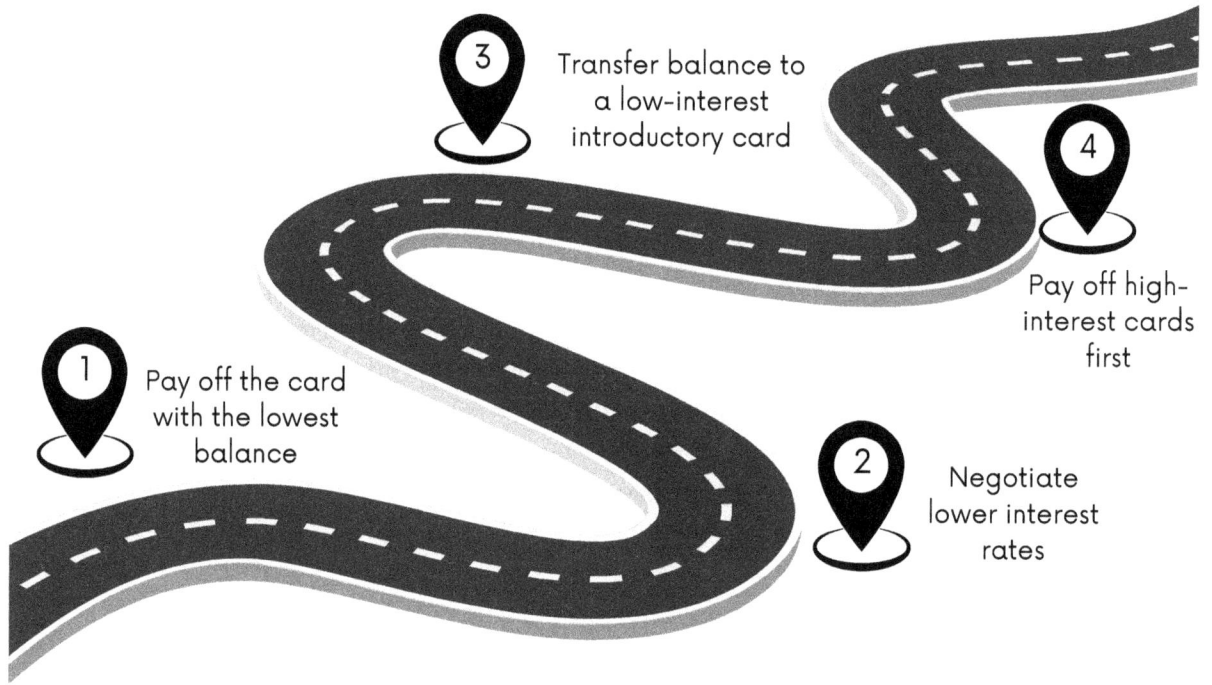

Do you have your GPS ready? Get ready for a few twists and turns on this route, which I call the "Blizzard Method" because we're about to unleash a flurry of tactics to obliterate your debt in record time. Remember, if the Blizzard ever makes it challenging to see the road ahead, you can always turn back and stick with the tried-and-true simplicity of snowballs and avalanches! Now, let's embark on this distinctive journey step by step.

 **Quick Win: Pay off the card with the lowest balance**

You've got to begin somewhere, and the simplest place to start is by paying off the card with the smallest balance. Not only will this boost your emotional well-being, but it will also grant you some breathing room to focus on improving the terms of those high-interest credit cards that seem determined to knock you off course.

The card I will pay off first is _____

It has a balance of _____

118

2 Pay Less: Negotiate lower interest rates

You're making fantastic progress towards paying off your first credit card – kudos to you! Now let's talk NEGOTIATION. I can sense the apprehension in the air as you contemplate making a U-turn. But before you do, take a close look at the graphic below. We have a group of four friends, and three of them have their hands up. Can you guess why? It's because they asked for a lower interest rate and successfully got it! And here's the kicker – none of these folks are negotiation experts. They simply asked politely and exercised patience. I want you to join that group with your hand held high too!

More than three in four cardholders who ask for a lower interest rate get it.

But you might be wondering, "How do I negotiate?" It's a great question! Here's the plan: Pick up your phone and dial the customer service number on the back of your credit card. Keep in mind that the higher your credit score and the better your history of on-time payments, the stronger your negotiation position. To make this process even simpler for you, I'm handing you a script. Go ahead and complete steps 3 and 4 as outlined, and then take a look at the script that follows. Adjust it to fit your style, get yourself pumped up, and then make that call!

The card with the highest interest rate is _____

It has a balance of _____ **and an interest rate of** _____

Don't limit yourself to just your highest interest rate card; invest a solid morning in making calls to all your credit card companies, politely requesting a lower rate.

3 **Save Big Time: Transfer balance to a low interest card**

Why settle for high interest rates when lower ones are within reach? It doesn't make sense. Let's say you shift a $5,000 balance from a credit card charging a 20% interest rate to a new card with a 1% introductory rate. Even with a 3% balance transfer fee, you'll pocket approximately $950 in annual interest savings. While the low rate will eventually revert to its regular level, you'll still enjoy significant savings in the meantime.

❌ Avoid the temptation of getting a new credit card and using it for purchases. Lock that new card away. Activate it and leave it there. Your primary focus is paying off your debt.

❌ Applying for too many cards can harm your credit score and trigger concerns. Aim for just one new card with the best available deal. If you have excellent credit, you might even secure a 0% interest card.

In an ideal scenario, you would pay off the new credit card before the introductory period concludes. However, even if you can't manage that, you'll still end up saving a significant amount of money. Now, you might be wondering, where can I find these fantastic credit card offers? Well, some of them might land in your mailbox or inbox as offers. Alternatively, you might need to do a bit of research. To start, visit **bankrate.com** and explore their credit card section.

Depending on your credit limit on the new card and your existing balances, you may have the option to transfer a portion or the entirety of your balance from one or more high-interest credit cards. Begin with the card carrying the highest interest rate (after any successful negotiations) and proceed systematically by addressing the balances with the next highest interest rates.

Here's my highest interest card _____

I will transfer this amount _____ **to the new card.**

It has an introductory interest rate of _____ **that expires on** _____

120

4 Finish the Job: Pay off Cards by Interest Rate

Take a moment to reflect on your accomplishments! You've successfully paid off the credit card with the lowest balance, negotiated for better interest rates, and even acquired a shiny new low-interest card to transfer part or all of your balance from high-interest cards. Your financial journey is on a smooth course now!

Now we're going to borrow the Avalanche playbook. Start by organizing your credit cards based on their interest rates. Channel extra payments towards the card with the highest interest rate, conquering it before moving on to the next in line. By implementing these strategies, you've transformed your journey through this detour into a turbocharged adventure.

Create a list outlining the sequence in which you'll tackle your debt. Start with the card with the lowest balance. And then sort by interest rate (from high to low).

Description	Balance	Minimum Payment	Interest Rate	Notes
1.				
2.				
3.				
4.				
5..				
6.				
7.				
8.				

In the upcoming pages, I'm providing you with a handy script to help negotiate better interest rates with your credit card companies. Plus, check out how Jordyn used Brenda's Blizzard Method to pay off debt fast. Finally, don't miss the nifty graph that lets you track your journey towards debt freedom!

Script to Negotiate a Better Annual Percentage Rate (APR)

<u>Before you Begin:</u> Decide on a reasonable interest rate that is acceptable to you. For example, if your credit card has an interest rate over 20%, getting it down to 12 to 15% seems reasonable. If you have other credit card offers, have that information in front of you.

YOU: Hi. My name is _____. I've been a customer for __ years. I've always paid my bills on time and I'd like to keep doing business with your company, but my APR rate seems high. I'd like to speak to someone who can do something about that. Is that something you can help me with, or can you please connect me with a supervisor who has the authority to offer a better APR?

CUSTOMER SERVICE REPRESENTATIVE: Please hold for a moment and I'll connect you with a supervisor (credit account specialist). [Remember to be Patient!]

SUPERVISOR: Hello, this is Sam. How can I help you?

YOU: Hi, my name is _____, and I'm interested in talking with someone about lowering my interest rate. Can you help me with that?

SUPERVISOR: Yes, I can discuss that with you. Can you tell me what your concerns are with your current rate?

YOU: Sure, but before we continue. Can I have your full name and direct telephone number in case we get disconnected?

SUPERVISOR: It's Sam Jones and my direct line is _____.

YOU: Thank you, Sam. I've been a good customer for ___ years, but I'm paying too much in interest. I'm working on paying off my credit card balances and I've been researching my options. I'd like to stay with _____ (credit card company), but I can find better interest rates from other companies. I've been offered balance transfer options with a _____% APR for ___months. Can you offer something similar, or at least bring the APR to something more reasonable?

> **"Debt is like any other trap, easy enough to get into, but hard enough to get out of."**
> **- Henry Wheeler Shaw**

If Sam refuses to negotiate:

YOU: Well, I'm disappointed. I'd hoped we could reach an agreement on this. I'll have to consider my other options and I may have to close my account.

SUPERVISOR: Thank you for contacting us. Is there anything else I can help you with?

YOU: No, thank you. I appreciate your patience.

If Sam offers an APR above your acceptable level:

YOU: Thank you for the offer, but I was hoping for a more competitive rate. Can you do any better? Something closer to the ___% mark?

SUPERVISOR: I'm sorry, but this is the best rate we can offer.

YOU: Okay, let me weigh my other options. I need to do some more research, but I appreciate your help.

If Sam offers an acceptable APR:

YOU: That's terrific! I'd like to go ahead and accept the offer. What are the steps I need to take and when will the new APR become effective?

SUPERVISOR: You'll notice the new APR on your next statement and we will send you confirmation. Can you verify your email address?

YOU: Yes, my email is _____. I really appreciate your help. Thank you so much! (Make sure to receive documentation.)

Notes

Jordyn faced a hefty $25,000 credit card debt spread across six different cards, each with its own unique balance and interest rate. They turned to Brenda's Blizzard Method, a strategic approach designed to navigate the treacherous terrain of debt quickly.

Jordyn embarked on their journey with determination and unwavering focus. The first step in their path was to tackle Card 1, the one with the lowest balance of $2,000. It was a small victory, but it provided them with the motivation they needed to press on.

As they diligently paid off Card 1, Jordyn transitioned to the next phase of the Blizzard Method – negotiation. With their excellent credit and the Money Road Trip's helpful script, they reached out to each credit card company to negotiate for better interest rates. Their efforts were fruitful as they successfully lowered the interest rates on several of their cards, smoothing the path to debt freedom.

But Jordyn's pursuit of financial freedom didn't stop there. They knew that a strategic move could further expedite their journey. Jordyn decided to apply for a new credit card, one with an enticing introductory offer – 0% interest for the first 18 months. Jordyn was approved for this amazing deal, allowing them to transfer high-interest balances and save substantially on interest charges.

As they continued to navigate the snowstorm of debt, Jordyn adhered to the final phase of the Blizzard Method. They prioritized paying off their remaining cards based on their interest rates, chipping away at the high-interest ones while managing the lower-interest ones with minimum payments.

With each card paid off, Jordyn's confidence grew, and the weight of debt began to lift. And as Jordyn continued their journey, they envisioned a future where they were not only debt-free but also empowered to make choices that aligned with their dreams and aspirations. Financial freedom was not just a destination for Jordyn; it represented a new beginning, a life unburdened by the chains of debt.

Total Debt Balance

$_____

100% _____

_____ 90%

80% _____

_____ 70%

60% _____

_____ 50%

40% _____

_____ 30%

20% _____

_____ 10%

0%

START

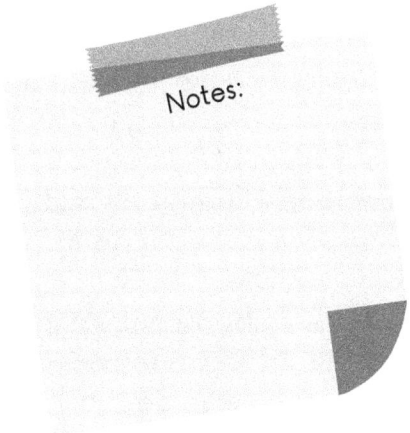

Notes:

Other Forms of Debt

Great news! You're approaching the end of your financial detour, and the good thing is, you can apply both the snowball and avalanche methods to tackle all your other debt, including mortgages, auto loans, student loans, and medical bills. However, it's essential to remember that unlike credit card debt, these types of financial obligations typically don't offer as much room for negotiation.

Imagine you're nearing the end of the detour, and right before the on-ramp, you spot two visitor information centers. The first one is all about student loan debt, and the second one covers medical debt. Now, it's entirely okay to breeze past both of these centers if you don't need the information today. You can always swing back later to pick it up.

You see, student loans and medical debt can be a bit trickier to navigate, and it's wise to be armed with the right information in advance. There are strategies to tackle each of these debt types, but without this knowledge, you might end up paying an unnecessary toll. Here's the inside scoop to keep your journey on the right track.

Navigating the Student Loan Maze

Obtaining student loans can seem like a breeze for young adults. It's as if an enticing offer of free money is dangling right in front of your eyes, promising a bright academic future with no immediate financial worries. After all, you don't have to start repaying until after graduation. But the truth is, millions of Americans find themselves on a decades-long journey to pay off their student loans, turning what seemed like a quick shortcut into yet another detour on the road to financial freedom.

Navigating the intricate terrain of student loan debt often feels like driving up a steep and winding mountain road. It's a journey marked by twists, turns, and moments of breathtaking uncertainty. This landscape continually evolves, with a complex web of federal programs and policies that can easily leave even the most informed borrowers feeling adrift.

As we embark on this expedition through the labyrinth of student loan debt, here are some strategies to consider. It's essential to remain vigilant, as new opportunities and programs emerge regularly.

☐ Consolidate your federal loans

If you've taken out multiple federal loans, you might be able to consolidate them into a single Direct Consolidation Loan. This simplifies your repayment by giving you one monthly payment and often extends the repayment period, reducing your monthly installment.

☐ Consider loan forgiveness programs

If you're working in public service or non-profit organizations, see if you qualify for the Public Service Loan Forgiveness Program. If you qualify and work for an eligible employer, after making 120 qualifying payments, the remaining loan balance is forgiven, tax-free. If you're a teacher, see if you qualify for Teacher Loan Forgiveness programs.

☐ Get help from your employer

Some employers, particularly in the public and non-profit sectors, offer Loan Repayment Assistance Programs (LRAPs) as part of their employee benefits. These programs provide financial assistance to help employees pay off their student loans more quickly.

☐ Automate your payments

Some lenders offer interest rate reductions when borrowers set up automatic payments. This can help lower the overall interest paid over the life of the loan.

☐ If your income is low, explore Income-Driven Repayment Plans

You might qualify for a program that calculates your monthly payment based on your income and family size. These plans can significantly lower your monthly payments and offer forgiveness after a specific period, usually 20 to 25 years.

⚠️ You might be able to get a lower interest rate by refinancing with private lenders. You'll get a new private loan with a lower interest rate that pays off your federal or other private student loans. Be cautious, as refinancing with private lenders means losing federal benefits like income-driven repayment options and loan forgiveness programs.

Feeling overwhelmed by all this information? You're not alone; these programs can be quite dynamic and ever-changing. To stay on top of your options, visit this federal website:

studentaid.gov

Taking the Pain out of Medical Bills

Medical debt, often referred to as the silent financial burden, looms over countless individuals and families in the United States. It's a shadow that can quickly turn into a storm, as medical bills pile up, insurance claims become disputes, and financial stability hangs in the balance. In fact, medical debt ranks as the leading cause of bankruptcy in the country. Even with health insurance, the lack of transparency and the complexities of healthcare coverage can lead to unexpected financial setbacks. But there are strategies to help you tackle medical debt and regain control of your financial future. Here are some effective ways to pay off medical debt as swiftly as possible:

☐ Check the bill for errors

Medical bills are filled with errors and outrageous costs for simple items. Get an itemized billing statement and an explanation of benefits (EOB) from the insurance company. Look for common mistakes, like
- Being billed more than once for the same service (duplicate billing)
- Incorrect patient information (name, social security number, insurance ID numbers
- Charges for canceled tests or procedures
- Inaccurate medication quantities

☐ Review your insurance policy

Make sure your bill and EOB match up with what your policy says it covers. If you think a service should have been covered call your insurance company.
- Your claim may have been denied due to an error (billing code) that can be easily corrected
- Your claim may have been denied for other reasons - treatment considered experimental or not medically necessary. You have the right to file an appeal (make sure your provider doesn't send the bill to collections while your claim is under appeal)

☐ Ask about financial assistance programs

If you still can't afford to pay the bill, ask if the hospital or facility has a financial assistance or charity programs available. You may qualify if:
- Your income is low
- You're unemployed
- You are not insured
- You still owe a large sum of money beyond what your insurance covers

☐ Negotiate to pay less

If you can't afford to pay your bill, call the billing department (be pleasant and patient) and tell them about your financial situation. Be ready to provide documentation. If you can afford to pay at least part of the bill in cash, try starting small by offering to settle the bill for 25% or 30% of the total in cash.
- If you can afford to pay the bill, ask if there is a prompt pay discount. Some providers may give you a discount up to 30% when you pay upfront

☐ Ask for a payment plan

Many hospitals and providers have programs that will allow you to pay your bill in monthly installments - frequently at 0% interest.

☐ Get help from an advocate

Get help from a medical bill advocate who can negotiate for you and possibly find billing errors you wouldn't be able to spot on your own. Advocates typically charge either by the hour or a percentage of the amount they're able to get reduced from the bill. If you're experiencing hardship, you may be able to get free of low-cost services through a nonprofit advocacy organization.

Bravo!

AWESOME!

Congratulations! You've conquered the debt chapter, and now this detour is officially in the rearview mirror. How does it feel to be back on the road to financial freedom? Let's take a moment to celebrate what you've accomplished during this scintillating discussion.

☐ You broke up with debt!

Oh, that breakup letter was divine! You poured your heart into it and finally severed that emotional attachment to debt. I'm absolutely thrilled for you. It's a significant step on your journey to financial freedom, and I couldn't be prouder of your determination and commitment.

☐ You have a winning strategy to pay off your debt.

You've embarked on quite the debt-detour adventure, learning about snowballs, avalanches, and blizzards! But what's even more crucial is that you've tailored a strategy that fits you like a glove. It takes into account your credit scores, spending habits, and individual personality. Armed with a well-thought-out plan and a toolkit filled with the right financial tools, you're well on your way to reaching the Summit, where you'll proudly plant your Debt-Free flag for all to see. Keep climbing!

☐ You're armed and ready to conquer any student loan debt and medical bills that might cross your path

Isn't it amazing how complex debt can be? But now, armed with some fundamental knowledge and resources, you're better equipped to explore avenues for reducing or eliminating your debt burden. The recurring theme here is clear: Research, negotiate, seek assistance, and strive to pay it off swiftly. Remember, you've got the skills and determination to tackle this challenge head-on!

Notes

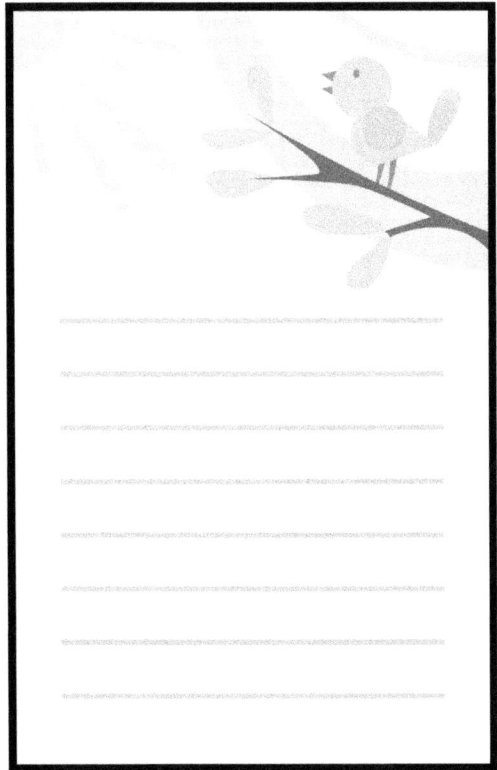

7

CROSS THE INVESTMENT BRIDGE

Cross the Investment Bridge

You're back on the road to financial freedom, but there are still challenges ahead, like the raging rivers and treacherous mountain passes. But no worries, because you can safely cross using bridges. Saving and investing are the bridges you'll be using to reach the other side.

Objectives

- To demonstrate the value of saving and investing
- To help you build a portfolio based on your timeframe
- To align your investments with sustainability values

Big Mission

Our mission is to help you build a savings and investment portfolio based on your timeframe and values.

To-do Checklist

- [ ] Learn the basics of investing
- [ ] Build your portfolio
- [ ] Start investing using low-fee options
- [ ] Make eco-smart decisions

Investing 101

You've mastered the essentials of financial freedom. Your mindset is solid, you've crafted a strategy to boost your income and cut expenses, and you're diligently chipping away at your debt. Now, here's a delightful predicament: you've got some surplus funds to work with. It's a wonderful challenge to tackle. While investing might seem complex, it doesn't have to be. Think of it as the bridge that connects your present situation to your desired financial future. This is your pathway to securing your future!

College Friends with Different Goals

Malik and Linh, two good friends from college, started their investing journeys at the age of 25. Malik, with a desire for security, invested $10,000 in a stable 3% savings account. Linh was drawn to the potential of the stock market and chose to invest her $10,000 in a low-fee index stock fund that averaged an annual return of 8%.

Now, take a look at the table below. It showcases the growth of $10,000 over time for both Malik and Linh. Brace yourself for an eye-opening revelation as we delve into their stories.

Growth of $10,000 over time

	Malik Savings - 3%	Linh Investments - 8%
5 Years	$11,593	$14,693
10 Years	$12,753	$19,062
15 Years	$14.027	$27,468
20 Years	$15,433	$46,610
25 Years	$16,697	$85,360
30 Years	$18,637	$153,763

As they started their investment journeys, Malik felt comforted by the steady, albeit modest, interest generated by his savings account. Linh, on the other hand, accepted the volatility of the stock market. She understood that while her investments would fluctuate, they had the potential for substantial growth over time.

Over the years, Malik saw his savings account grow steadily, but the pace was slow compared to what he hoped to achieve. Still, he remained committed to his financial goals and believed in the security his savings account provided.

Linh's investment journey was filled with thrilling moments. She experienced market highs and lows, but her portfolio consistently outperformed a traditional savings account. Linh was careful not to let emotions guide her decisions, relying on her research and long-term perspective.

At age 40, 15 years after that $10,000 investment, Malik had grown his savings account to $14,027. His approach saw his money grow, but it didn't even keep up with inflation. Linh, now 40 as well, had experienced the full spectrum of market dynamics. Her initial $10,000 investment had grown to an impressive $27,468. While she had encountered moments of uncertainty, her diversified portfolio had weathered market downturns and emerged stronger.

As they reflected on their investment journeys, Malik and Linh realized that their choices had led to different outcomes. Malik had prioritized stability and had achieved slow but consistent growth. Linh, on the other hand, had embraced volatility and reaped the rewards of higher returns.

"Risk comes from not knowing what you're doing"
- Warren Buffet

Let's Talk Risk

Here's the fundamental truth: many people find investing intimidating simply because they don't know how to navigate it. So what should be your first investment? Knowledge! Let's begin our exploration by addressing the concept of risk.

You may have noticed the stark difference between Malik and Linh's investment performances. After 25 years, Malik's $10,000 grows to $16,697, while Linh's identical investment in stock funds skyrockets to $85,360. That's a staggering difference of $68,663.

The takeaway here? When dealing with short-term investments, safety and accessibility are your companions, and slow growth is fine. But relying solely on conservative savings plans won't lead to much long-term growth. In fact, it can be a risky move as inflation gradually erodes the value of your earnings.

Now, imagine you're sitting across from a professional financial advisor, and they ask you to complete a risk assessment quiz. Your score could determine whether you settle for a low-risk low-return portfolio or embrace more volatile investments that have the potential for higher rates of return. Here's the catch: these risk assessments often miss the mark. Why? Because risk is a complex, multi-dimensional concept heavily influenced by recent experiences. If you've just weathered a stock market storm, you're more likely to lean towards caution. But during a bull market, marked by stock market victories, you might fancy a wild ride.

On the next page, you'll see an investment pyramid, your guide to risk levels across different investment types. So, how do you navigate this intricate landscape? Diversify your investments across various asset classes and keep a watchful eye on your investment horizon.

Start small and figure out your investing quirks. If market turbulence tends to make you jittery, consider taming that impulse or adjusting your risk level accordingly. Keep in mind that every investor has their unique tendencies and priorities, and your investment strategy should cater to your individual road trip.

Generally, what is your investing preferences? (select one)

O   O   O

Low-interest   Balanced   Aggressive
Savings   funds   investing

```
                                              ↑   High
                                                  Risk
                      /\
                     /  \
                    / Options \
                   / Futures  \
                  / Commodities \
                 / Individual Stocks \
                /──────────────────\
               /                    \
              /   Mutual Funds        \
             /    Corporate Bonds      \
            / Exchange-Traded Funds (ETFs)\
           /    Foreign Exchange          \
          /     Balanced Funds             \
         / Real Estate Investment Trusts (REITs)\
        /──────────────────────────────────\
       /                                      \
      /         Fixed Annuities                \
     /          Municipal Bonds                  \
    /           Treasury Bonds                     \
   /            Money Market Funds                  \
  /         Certificates of Deposit (CDs)            \   Low
 /              Savings Accounts                      \  Risk
/──────────────────────────────────────────────────\ ↓
```

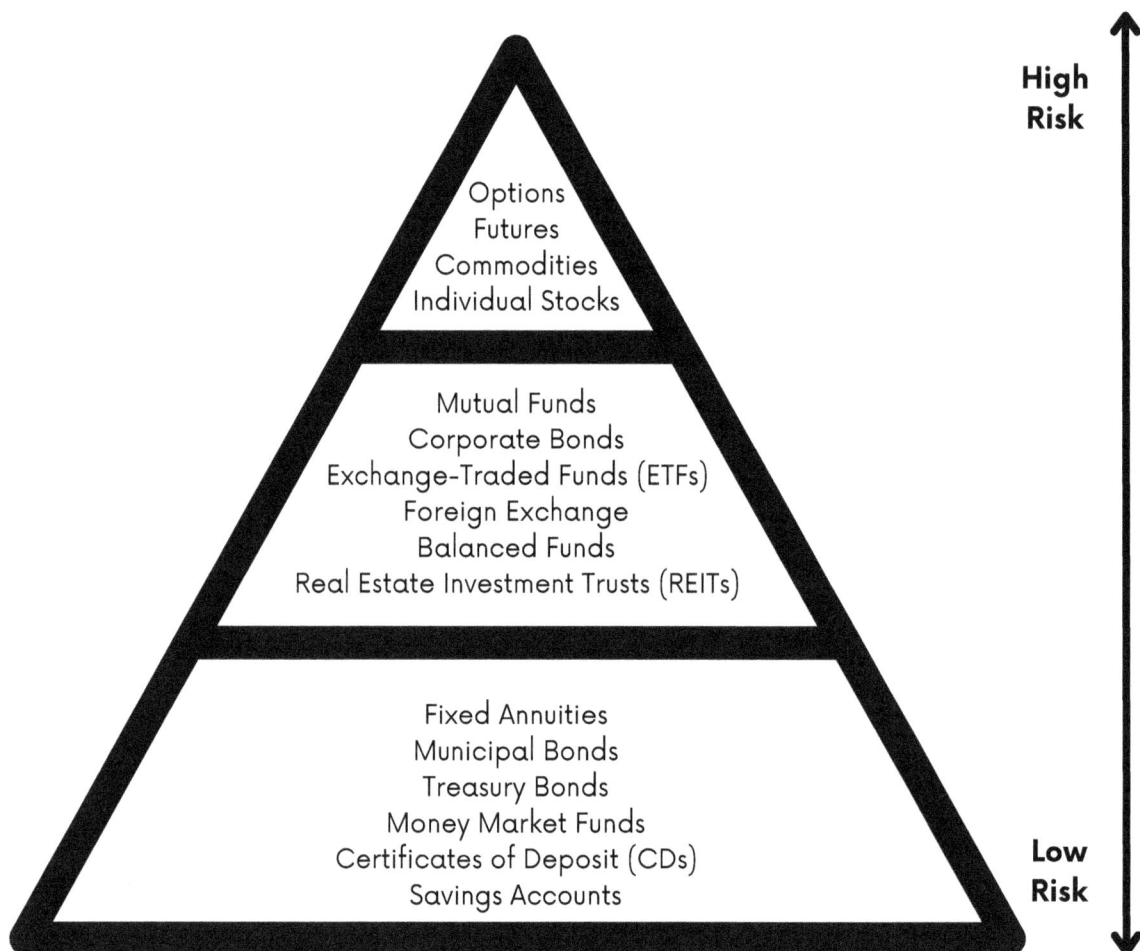

That's a lot of jargon and financial terms! But let's simplify things a bit and focus on the relationship between risks and returns. It's a fundamental principle to understand. Generally, low-risk investments tend to yield lower returns, but they offer more assurance and stability during economic downturns. As you ascend the investment pyramid, the risks increase, and with that, the potential for both substantial gains and significant losses.

The pyramid provides examples of various types of funds by risk level. Notably, there's a missing piece in the puzzle—speculative funds. These investments are known for their high degree of risk and the potential for substantial gains or losses. Speculative funds often lack a consistent track record of stable returns and may involve uncertain or speculative factors, making them more susceptible to market volatility and unpredictability. While they can be enticing, they should be approached with caution, especially by those new to investing.

Perhaps you noticed the absence of cryptocurrencies in the pyramid? At the time of this writing, crypto is considered a speculative investment. Think of it like an unpredictable game where the rules are still being written. Cryptocurrencies are fairly new and their value can swing dramatically based on market trends and investor enthusiasm, often influenced by social media.

The key here is that crypto isn't like traditional, more stable investments. It's not backed by physical assets or as heavily regulated, which adds to its unpredictability. While it offers the potential for high returns, it also comes with the risk of significant drops, including the total loss of funds. If you put money into a speculative investment, make it a very small percentage of your portfolio, and understand you may lose it all.

Great job on wading through Investment 101. Let's pause for a zen moment. Draw a route through this maze, leading to the pot of gold at its center.

Fill up your Money Bags

I'm totally confident in your potential as a savvy investor. The secret to effective investing? Remove emotion from the equation. When the market dips and panic is in the air, keep your cool. This is often the prime moment for buying undervalued stocks as others hastily sell. Conversely, when the market is booming and everyone is buying, consider holding or selling assets that may be overvalued. Remember, markets naturally ebb and flow - staying calm is your superpower.

Ready to simplify and thrive? Here are three strategies you can use to stay calm in the wild world of investing.

- ☐ Make it automatic - make regular contributions regardless of what is happening in the economy.

- ☐ Think in phases - make investment decisions based on when you will need to access the money.

- ☐ Limit your choices - commit to a select group of core funds to avoid the temptation of chasing after the latest "hot" stock.

The table below offers suggested types of investments by timeframe. You'll see that lower-risk investments are recommended for shorter durations, whereas higher-risk options are more suited to longer timeframes, allowing them to weather market fluctuations and capitalize on growth potential.

Timeframe	Suggested Types of Investments
Emergency (less than a year)	High-yield savings accounts, Money market accounts, Short-term CDs
Short-term (1 to 3 years)	Short-term bonds, Treasury bills, Conservative mutual funds
Mid-term (4 to 9 years)	Balanced mutual funds, Index funds, Dividend stocks, Real estate
Long-term (10 or more years)	Stocks, Stock mutual funds, ETFs, Long-term bonds, Retirement accounts (401k, IRA)

That was quite a bit to take in, wasn't it? When we start looking at long-term financial planning, things can sometimes feel a bit hazy. So, let's bring it back to the real world – focusing on when you might need (or want) to access your funds. You've been diligently contributing, but eventually, there will come a time to withdraw. To make it simpler, let's categorize your savings into three distinct 'money bags': Security, Dream Fund, and Retirement. Each serves a unique purpose in your financial journey.

 Fill up your Security Money Bag (1 year of expenses)

Let's dive into the first step of our financial journey – achieving financial security. The goal here is simple yet crucial: keep your savings safe and easily accessible. It may not be the most thrilling part of your financial strategy, but it's fundamental.

One of the best perks of the trusty traditional bank is the insurance it offers – a safety net that's hard to find elsewhere. As of 2024, the Federal Deposit Insurance Corporation (FDIC) insures up to $250,000 per depositor, per bank, per account type. So, if the bank goes under, your money doesn't go with it.

You can keep all your money in the same place, or if you prefer, mix it up a bit. For instance, you could put half of your funds into a 6-month Certificate of Deposit (CD) for a slightly better interest rate. The rest can go into an online bank and a local credit union or bank.

The only hitch? Taxes. The interest you earn counts as taxable income. But don't worry – as you progress in your financial journey, you'll encounter more options that are kinder to your tax bill. So, let's kickstart this process. Write down your savings goal and how you plan to distribute it across different accounts. You might not have all the details figured out just yet, but a ballpark figure is a great beginning.

▷ Discover the best interest rates for savings accounts and CDs at **bankrate.com**.

My Plans for my Security Money Bag

Amount I need to cover 12 months of expenses: _____

Name of Investment	Goal Amount	Current Level
TOTAL		

Invest in your Dreams

I'll let you in on a little secret – until not so long ago, I had never heard of a 'Dream Fund.' It was in David Bach's book, "Smart Women Finish Rich," where I first came across the term, and gosh, was it a revelation! So, what exactly is a Dream Fund? It's your ticket to freedom, your chance to make choices driven by pure joy. It's the spark that lights up your deepest desires, turning dreams into reality. Whether it's buying that cozy cabin by the lake, taking a year off to travel the globe, adopting a child, launching your own business, mastering a new skill, or anything else that sets your heart aflutter – that's what a Dream Fund is for.

A particular story from that book resonated deeply with me. It described a woman who, despite not being clear about her dreams, committed to building a fund for them. I related to her; I too was diligently contributing to my Dream Fund, albeit with foggy dreams. Then, unexpectedly, life took a sharp turn, and suddenly, my dreams crystallized before me. In that moment of transformation, I was immensely grateful for having saved faithfully, even when my end goals were yet to be defined.

This could be the perfect moment to flip back to chapter 2. That's where you began sculpting your vision, plotting your journey, and identifying your dream. You also arranged your values in order of importance. Here's the crucial part about the Dream Fund – it's a repository for your aspirations, and the amount you aim for reflects your comfort with risk. What exactly does this mean? Consider the broad spectrum of financial freedom – ranging from 1x to 25x your annual expenses. That's quite a spread. For example, if your yearly expenses are around $50,000, your financial freedom scale could range from just over $50,000 to nearly $1.25 million!

Keep the following factors in mind as you grow your Dream Fund. Your goal is uniquely yours and may shift with life's changes. Exciting stories are coming up to inspire you. And remember, it's entirely possible to build your Dream Fund while you're already on the path to realizing your dreams!

Lifestyle Goals and Aspirations	The more ambitious your goals and aspirations, the more money you'll need to save.
Income Streams and Assets	If you plan to continue working, have other income streams, or assets you can sell, you'll need less money.
Age and Life Stage	If you're decades away from accessing your retirement funds, you might want a bigger cushion.
Dependents and Family Obligations	If you have family depending on you, your family's needs might require a larger Dream Fund.
Health Conditions	If you'll need health insurance coverage or have medical conditions that require treatment, you'll need a larger fund.

Amanda, in her early 30s, had always been a diligent saver. She started her Dream Fund without a clear vision of what it was for, just a sense that it was something important. Working in the corporate world had provided her with a stable income, but recently, she found herself feeling restless, yearning for something more fulfilling.

Her turning point came unexpectedly during a wellness retreat she attended on a whim. The retreat was a revelation. Nestled in a serene, mountainous landscape, it offered a range of classes, and Amanda tried them all. Each session left her feeling more rejuvenated, more alive.

As she returned to her daily grind, the contrast between her job and the experience at the retreat became starkly apparent. The dream began to take shape in her mind – she wanted to delve into the world of wellness, not just as a participant, but as an expert. She imagined herself guiding others towards healthier, more balanced lives, just as she had been guided at the retreat.

But to make this dream a reality, Amanda knew she needed a solid plan. She dove into researching wellness certifications, including Yoga Teacher Training, Nutrition and Holistic Health Coaching, and potentially Ayurvedic practices. She mapped out a two-year journey: the first year to balance her corporate job with part-time classes, allowing her to explore various wellness paths and network with industry professionals. The second year would be a deep dive – quitting her job to focus entirely on gaining certifications, apprenticing with top instructors, and drafting a business plan. For this, she calculated needing about $80,000 in her Dream Fund.

Looking at her fund, which had reached $40,000, Amanda felt a blend of excitement and apprehension. She was halfway to her goal, and estimated it would take another three years to fully fund her dream. Undeterred, she considered part-time work or a wellness-related side hustle, not only to grow her fund but also to gain valuable experience in her chosen field. This pragmatic approach kept her dream vivid and within reach, blending practical steps with her burgeoning passion for wellness.

In Amanda's mind, the vision of her future self grew clearer with each passing day. She saw herself leading yoga classes in a sunlit studio, conducting workshops on holistic living, and perhaps even starting her own wellness blog or podcast. The dream was no longer a distant, hazy image; it had colors and shapes, it had a timeline, and most importantly, it had Amanda's heart and soul woven into it.

Kimani Family Reunion

Meet the Kimani family – John and Wanjiku, along with their two children, Makena and Njau. Their dream was one of unity: to bring Wanjiku's parents from Kenya to live with them in the United States. For the Kimanis, this dream was more than just a reunion; it was about cultural preservation, family bonds, and intergenerational support. They envisioned Wanjiku's parents enriching their children's lives with stories, traditions, and the Swahili language, while also playing a pivotal role in their upbringing.

To turn this dream into reality, the Kimanis formulated a detailed plan for their Dream Fund. Their budgeting became a family affair, with even the children contributing ideas on how to save. John took up additional freelance projects, tapping into his skills as a graphic designer, while Wanjiku, a school teacher, started a small weekend catering business, specializing in Kenyan cuisine.

The biggest challenge was the financial logistics of their goal. They calculated the costs: immigration and legal fees for the citizenship process, travel funds, and ensuring a comfortable living place for their extended family. They set their goal at $120,000 for the entire process.

Every night, the family sat around the dinner table, updating their savings chart. The children would excitedly add stickers for each milestone reached, their eyes gleaming with the prospect of having their grandparents close. John and Wanjiku often found themselves up late, discussing their plans and reminiscing about their childhood in Kenya.

As months turned into years, their Dream Fund grew, fueled by their hard work and community support. Finally, the day arrived when they reached their goal. Emotions ran high as they started the immigration process for Wanjiku's parents. The thought of their children growing up with their grandparents, just as they had, filled them with overwhelming happiness and gratitude.

The Kimani's story was one of perseverance, love, and the unbreakable bond of family. Their Dream Fund was more than just a savings account; it was a testament to their dedication to family, heritage, and the future of their children, bridging continents and weaving a richer tapestry for their lives.

Your Dream Fund may encompass a variety of aspirations - from a house down payment, to a Caribbean getaway, kickstarting a side hustle, or helping a relative with a loan. When this mix starts feeling overwhelming, consider dividing your grand Dream Fund into smaller, focused "money bags." This approach makes your goals feel more attainable. Below, use the provided graphic to list your dreams alongside the target dates by which you want the funds ready to make these dreams a reality.

Dream Fund

Dream: _____
1 **Target Date:** _____

Dream: _____
2 **Target Date:** _____

Dream: _____
3 **Target Date:** _____

Embarking on the journey to your dreams can feel like juggling several colorful balloons, each with its own destination. For those dreams just around the corner, say within the next year, park your funds in a trusty savings account where they're safe and sound. As for the dreams that are a bit further down the road, nailing down the exact price tag and vision might be more like trying to catch a cloud – a bit elusive, but oh-so-exciting!

Now, if your grandest dream is sailing into financial independence, where work becomes a choice rather than a necessity, well, you've got an adventure ahead! But remember, every epic journey is made up of smaller, thrilling excursions. Sprinkle your Dream Fund path with these mini-milestones to keep the momentum going.

While your dream map may have multiple stops and timelines, think of your investments like a well-packed suitcase – just a few essential items, not the entire closet! Too many accounts in too many places can turn your dream quest into a bit of a treasure hunt. So, keep it simple and sweet.

On the table below, chart out the investments for your Dream Fund, along with when you hope they'll come to life, and where you currently stand. If you're starting with a blank page, no worries – that's the start of every great story, and exactly why this book is your travel companion! Scribble down some ideas, and let your dreams take root!

My Plans for my Dream Fund

Amount I want in my Fund: _____

Name of Investment	Goal Amount	Current Level
TOTAL		

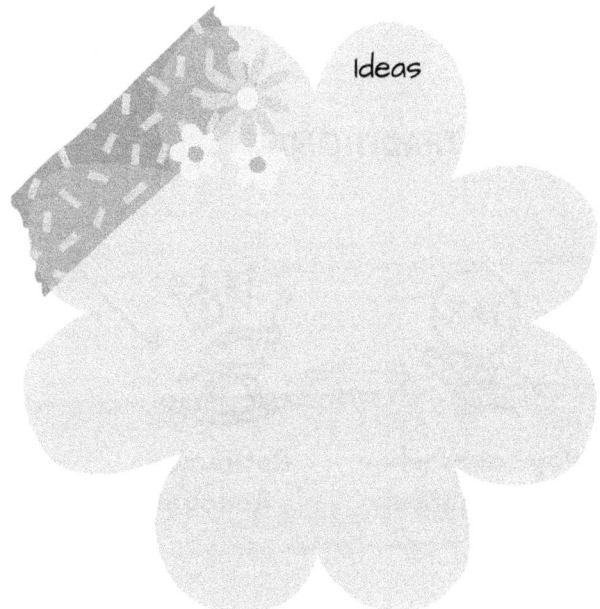

Thoughts

Ideas

As we wrap up our Dream Fund chat, here's a quick tax tip: Most investments outside retirement accounts face federal, state, and local taxes. But there are some options with tax advantages. Take Treasury bills, for example – they dodge state and local taxes (but not federal tax). Municipal bonds can be free from federal taxes, and if you're in the issuing state, maybe state and local taxes too. Real estate? That's a different playbook, with some perks after federal deductions. Don't let taxes dampen your dream plans. If slicing your tax bill is high on your list, a chat with a tax pro can be super helpful to navigate these waters.

"In this world, nothing is certain except death and taxes."
- Benjamin Franklin

Load up your Retirement

We've arrived at the pinnacle of our financial journey – retirement planning! If you're one of the lucky few with a pension, that's fantastic – it's a rare perk these days. However, for most, a pension isn't in the cards. Instead, we rely on company-sponsored plans or personal savings strategies. One of the biggest perks of stashing your cash in retirement accounts is the tax benefits they offer. There are two main types of accounts to consider: Traditional and Roth. The key difference? It's all about the timing of tax payments. Let's break it down.

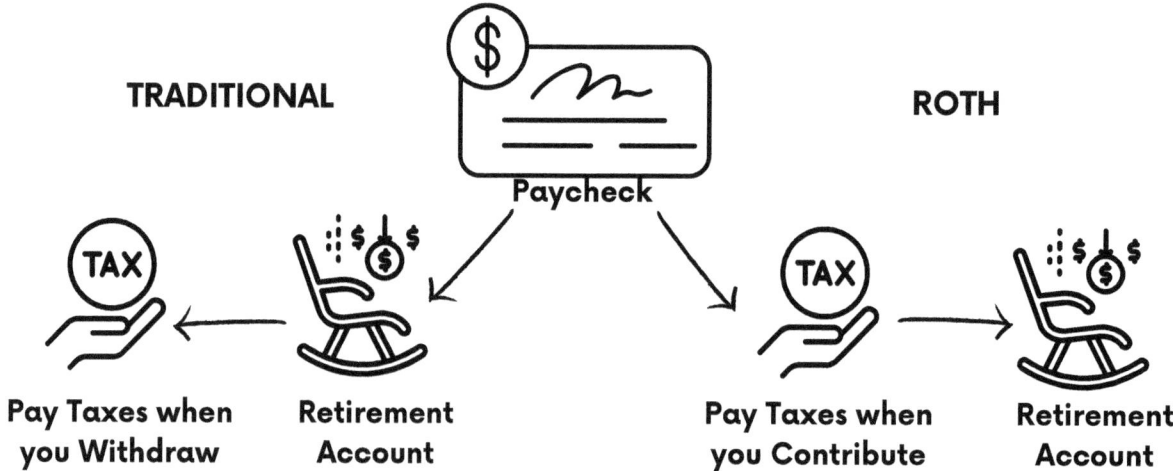

TRADITIONAL   **Paycheck**   **ROTH**

Pay Taxes when you Withdraw | **Retirement Account** | **Pay Taxes when you Contribute** | **Retirement Account**

The timing of when you pay taxes on your investments definitely matters! Imagine you're in your 20s, kickstarting your career. Chances are, you're in a lower tax bracket now than you will be later on. In this scenario, opting for a Roth account can be a smart move. You'll pay taxes upfront, but then your money grows tax-free for decades. When it's time to withdraw, that money is all yours, with no tax bill attached. It's a savvy strategy for those early in their earning years.

You may hear the following tip: If you anticipate being in a lower tax bracket during retirement, a traditional retirement account is your best bet. On the flip side, if you expect to be in a higher tax bracket later on, or you prefer tax-free withdrawals, then go for a Roth. Predicting future tax brackets is like trying to read a crystal ball – it's nearly impossible. Life's uncertainties and the unknowns of investment returns make it tricky. The Roth offers a kind of certainty: pay your taxes now, enjoy tax-free growth, and don't worry about taxes on withdrawals. No guesswork required.

Employer-Sponsored Programs vs. Individual Retirement Accounts

Just as you've gotten the hang of traditional versus Roth accounts, the world of retirement savings throws a few more terms into the mix. If you're enjoying an employer match on your retirement contributions, you're likely familiar with your company's traditional plan. While there's a variety of company-sponsored plans out there, the most prevalent is the 401(k). Generally, the rules governing 401(k)s are a good indicator of the regulations that apply to other similar types of plans.

Private companies typically offer a 401(k) retirement plan, but various organizations use different retirement plan models. Non-profit organizations often have 403(b) plans, state and local governments use 457 plans, and federal employees along with uniformed service members are provided with the Thrift Savings Plan (TSP).

Your employer-sponsored plan and personal IRA come with their own sets of rules and limits. The table below outlines the 2024 limits, but keep in mind these can vary annually, often adjusting for inflation. Let's dive into key information:

🔑 You can contribute to your employer-sponsored plan regardless of your income level. This is true for both traditional and Roth 401(k)s.

🔑 Five years after the date you opened your account, you can take your **contributions** out of your Roth IRA. But your earnings will be taxed if you withdraw them before age 59½.

🔑 The Roth IRA is not subject to Required Minimum Distributions (RMDs). If you're contributing to a Roth 401(k), you can roll it over into a Roth IRA later on. This strategy allows you to bypass the RMDs that apply to the 401(k).

	Employer-Sponsored Plans 401(k)	Individual Retirement Accounts (IRAs)
Roth options?	Some companies	Yes
2024 contribution levels	$23,000 (under age 50) $30,500 (50 and older)	$7,000 (under age 50) $8,000 (50 and older)
2024 Income limits to be eligible to contribute	No limits, even for Roth 401(k)	Singles - $146,000 (phase-out range to $161,000) Couples - $230,000 (phase-out range to $240,000
Required Minimum Distribution (RMD)	age 73	age 73 for traditional IRA (no RMD for Roth IRA)
Penalties for early withdrawal (before age 59½)	Early withdrawals are subject to a 10% penalty and regular income tax. There are some exceptions.	Traditional IRA - early withdrawals typically incur a 10% penalty and are taxed as ordinary income. Roth IRA - Contributions can be taken out at any time.

Wow, that was a heap of info to take in! Now, let's steer back towards our main destination: FINANCIAL FREEDOM. All set to go? Here are two top recommendations to propel you forward, plus one extra Super Challenge for the daring!

★ Front load your retirement account. Put as much in at as fast as you can while you're younger. You will be amazed by its growth. And then, you can slow down or even halt contributions.

★ Heavily invest in Roth funds. If your employer offers a Roth 401(k), go for it. If not, invest in the traditional 401(k) AND a personal Roth IRA.

★ *Challenge* **MAKE IT A RACE to $100,000 in your Retirement Account**

Why am I nudging you towards that $100,000 milestone in your retirement account? Let's see the magic it can do! We'll explore how your money grows over time with two different rates of return – 7% for a balanced fund and 10% for a fund that tracks the stock market. Get ready for some eye-opening insights!

Growth of $100,000 over Time

Value	7% annual rate of return	10% annual rate of return
Year 0	$100,000	$100,000
Year 10	$196,715	$259,374
Year 20	$386,968	$672,750
Year 30	$771,226	$1,744,940

Now what do you think about this challenge? Are you up for it? Remember, the numbers above assume that your retirement account doesn't see a single extra contribution beyond the initial $100,000. Just picture the potential growth when you keep adding to it!

Are you feeling a mix of excitement and wonder at how $100,000 could blossom into $1.7 million without additional contributions? That's the magic of compound interest at work. With this, you're not just earning interest on the initial $100,000 (the principal) but also on the interest that accumulates over time.

It does seem a bit like a financial wizardry, doesn't it? Let's demystify it with another concept: The Rule of 72. This rule offers a straightforward way to gauge the time it takes for your investment to double in value at a given interest rate. Simply divide 72 by your annual rate of return, and voilà – you get an estimated number of years for your money to double. This rule really puts the power of compound interest into perspective!

- An investment that earns a 7% annual return will double in 10.3 years (72/7).
- An investment that earns a 10% annual return will double in 7.2 years (72/10).

How much do you think you'll need? Keep in mind that early withdrawals, typically before age 59½, often come with penalties (with the exception of your Roth IRA contributions). So, if you have many years of investing ahead and can handle the market's ups and downs, it might be wise to adopt a more aggressive investment approach initially. As you approach the age when you plan to start withdrawals, shifting to a more conservative strategy can help safeguard your investments.

My Plans for my Retirement Fund

My target retirement fund goal: _____

Name of Retirement Fund	Type (Trad/Roth)	Goal Amount	Current Level
TOTAL			

Navigating through Security funds, Dream funds, and Retirement funds might feel like a juggling act. The key? Simplify and prioritize. It's not about trying to fill every money bag all at once. Instead, create a focused plan and adhere to it. Let's take a page from Emily's playbook to see how she effectively manages it.

Emily's Plan Takes Shape

Meet Emily, a vibrant 26-year-old with a spark in her eyes and a plan in her pocket. Emily's journey towards financial freedom is a balancing act of dreams, responsibilities, and savvy financial moves. Living in her cozy shared apartment, she's already achieved her first significant milestone – saving six months' worth of expenses in her Security Fund.

Her daily life is a harmonious blend of work, creativity, and careful financial planning. Each morning, as the city wakes up, Emily sips coffee from her favorite mug, a reminder of her small yet significant choices towards frugality. Working in digital marketing, she's not only carving out a career but also diligently building her financial future. She takes full advantage of her employer's 401(k) match, a step that solidifies her commitment to a secure retirement.

Yet, Emily's aspirations extend beyond the walls of security. Her next ambitious goal is to grow her Security Fund to cover a full year's expenses, doubling down on her assurance against life's unforeseen twists. Her disciplined savings plan is a testament to her resolve, as she meticulously sets aside a portion of her income towards this goal.

Once this objective is reached, Emily plans to rechannel her savings strategy. The idea is to split her contributions – half will accelerate her retirement savings, leveraging the power of compound interest in her 401(k). The other half will be a bridge to her dreams, nourishing her Dream Fund dedicated to a backpacking adventure across Europe. This fund isn't just about travel; it's a canvas for her dreams, where each contribution adds a stroke of possibility to her vision of wandering through cobblestone streets, indulging in new cuisines, and absorbing the diverse cultures.

In Emily's journey, every financial decision is a stitch in the tapestry of her life. Her approach is more than mere savings; it's about weaving a future that balances the solidity of security with the vibrant hues of her aspirations. Her story isn't just about numbers in a bank account; it's about crafting a life that's rich in experiences, secure in stability, and abundant in possibilities.

It always SEEMS IMPOSSIBLE until IT'S DONE

You know what? You've absolutely wowed me with your progress! Now, let's use this page as your financial map. Jot down your goals for each of your key funds: your Security Fund, Dream Fund, and Retirement Fund. Let's bring all these pieces together into a clear and inspiring picture of your financial future!

Security Fund Goal: _____   Target Date: _____

Dream Fund Goal: _____   Target Date: _____

Retirement Fund Goal: _____   Target Date: _____

TOTAL

Notes

How to Invest

Navigating the world of investing can seem daunting at first, especially if you're used to the simplicity of opening an online savings account. The great news? Self-directed investing has become more accessible and user-friendly than ever before. However, the wide array of choices available can make it tricky to figure out where to begin. Let's dive into how you can smartly invest, keeping more money in your wallet and making it work for you.

Can I do it Myself?

Certainly! Within your employer-sponsored retirement plan, your options are confined to the investments offered in the plan. However, beyond this limitation, you have the freedom to manage your own financial portfolio. I strongly encourage you to take advantage of this opportunity to take control of your personal investments!

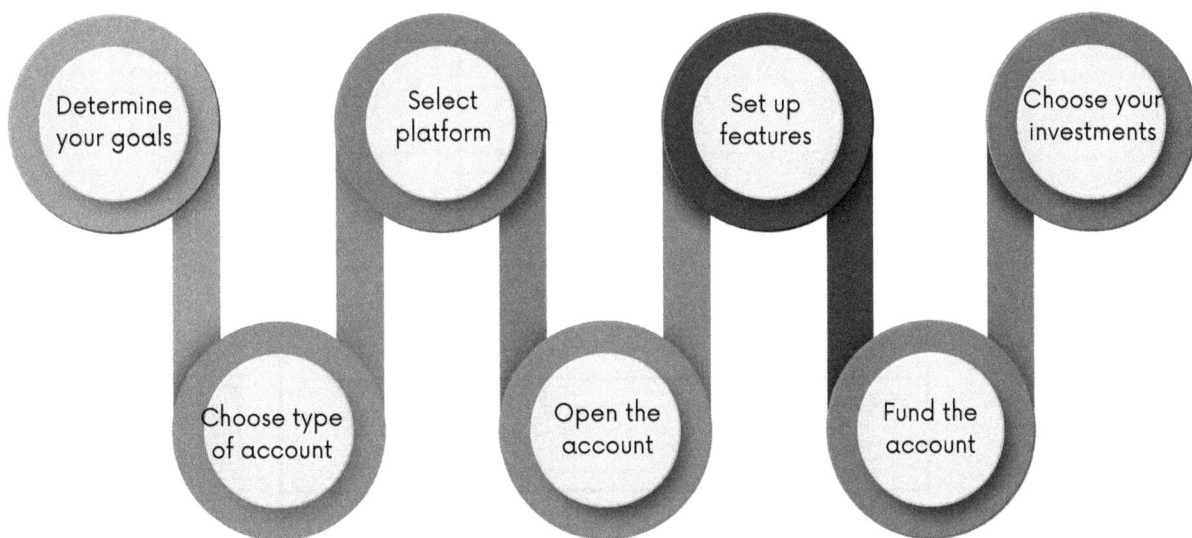

Determine your goals → Choose type of account → Select platform → Open the account → Set up features → Fund the account → Choose your investments

1 Determine your goals

You've just zipped through a primer on investing with your timeline in mind. Now, it's time to set a clear goal for the funds in this account. Is it earmarked for a down payment on a dream home, or perhaps for that once-in-a-lifetime trip around the globe? Or are you laser-focused on reaching your ultimate financial independence milestone? Reflect on what you're aiming for and the timeline you envision to achieve these goals.

2 **Choose type of account**

What kind of account suits your needs best? Essentially, you have three primary options: (1) a brokerage account for investing and trading in a taxable environment; (2) a retirement account like a Roth or Traditional IRA for long-term savings; or (3) an education fund, such as a 529 account, for future educational expenses.

Pause for a moment to consider your objectives. Jot down your goals and identify which type of account aligns best with each one. This exercise will help clarify your financial path and the tools you'll use to walk it.

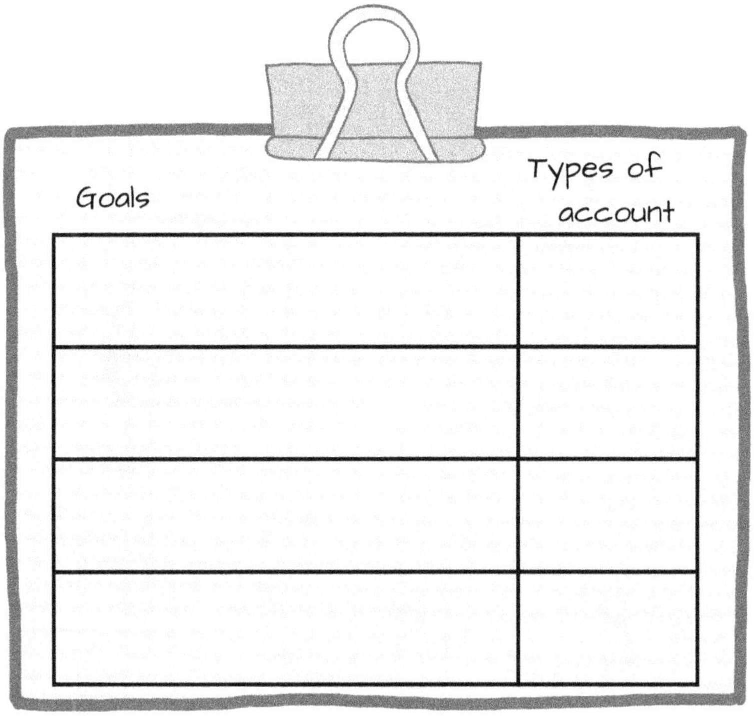

Goals	Types of account

3 **Select the platform**

Now's the moment for some homework, focusing on aspects like fees, minimum balance requirements, the range of available investments, and customer service quality. Your choices span traditional brokers, robo-advisors, or online brokerage platforms. Since fees can significantly impact your returns, it's wise to consider robo-advisors, which typically offer lower fees. A great resource for starting your research is NerdWallet.

bit.ly/nerdwalletrobo

4 **Open the account**

You've made your selection and now it's time to open an account. You'll typically need your Social Security Number (SSN), a government-issued ID, employment information, and bank account details for transfers.

5 **Set up features**

Your next step is to designate the features you'd like, such as automatic deposits, dividend reinvestment plans, or alerts.

6 **Fund the account**

Transfer money from your bank account to your investment account. This could be a one-time transfer or regular transfers.

7 **Choose your investments**

The last step in setting up your investment strategy, and one you'll continue to engage with, is selecting your investments. Consider your timeline and the options available to you. Whenever possible, opt for index funds or Exchange-Traded Funds (ETFs). These funds are designed to automatically track market indices and typically come with the added benefit of low fees.

Notes

Let's Talk Fees

Starting out in investing can be a bit daunting. It's tempting to hand over control to an advisor or a fund manager, but I encourage you to dive into managing your own finances. Understanding the impact of fees is crucial, and I'll show you the significant savings you can achieve with low-fee index funds.

Let's break down the key differences between managed funds and index funds:

- **Managed Funds**: These are actively managed by professionals who frequently buy and sell stocks or other assets, aiming to beat the market. Their expense ratios usually range from 0.50% to over 1.50%.
- **Index Funds**: These funds are designed to mirror the performance of a specific market index, like the S&P 500, through passive management with minimal trading. Their expense ratios are much lower, typically between 0.02% to 0.20%.

Now, let's address the myth of performance. Fund managers often justify high fees by claiming their expertise leads to superior returns. However, the reality is that consistently outperforming the market is extremely challenging, if not impossible.

The Buffett Bet

Dreaming of a cool $1,000,000 by outsmarting the stock market? Sounds tempting, right? Warren Buffett, a legendary investor, once threw down the gauntlet to fund managers to see if they could outperform the market.

In 2007, Buffett wagered $1 million that over a ten-year period, an S&P 500 index fund would outperform a collection of actively managed hedge funds. He argued that the high fees charged by active fund managers would make it difficult for them to outdo the market consistently over an extended period.

Buffett selected a low-cost Vanguard S&P 500 index fund, while Protégé Partners, a New York City money management firm, chose five hedge funds to represent the active management side. The bet ran from 2008 to 2017.

The result? The index fund significantly outperformed the hedge funds. By the end of 2017, Buffett's chosen index fund had an average annual return of 7.1%, compared to the 2.2% average annual return of the hedge funds selected by Protégé Partners. The winnings were donated to charity, and Buffett's success in this bet reinforced his long-held belief in the value of low-cost, passive index fund investing.

Run the Numbers

Over extended periods, the ability of managed funds to match the performance of index funds falls short. One key reason is the significant impact of their higher fees on your returns. At first glance, the difference in fees – say, 0.03% for an index fund versus 1.0% for a managed fund – might seem trivial. But don't let the seemingly small gap fool you. The long-term effect of these fees on your investment returns can be substantial.

Let's take a closer look using a practical example. Consider Vanguard's S&P 500 ETF, a classic index fund with a low expense ratio of 0.03%. Compare this with a typical managed fund charging 1.0%. The difference is just 0.97%, but over time, this can have a profound impact on your investment's growth.

The table below outlines a scenario in which you invest $50,000 in two different funds, each earning an average annual return of 7%. The sole distinction between them lies in their fee structures. Observe how these fees influence the growth of your investment over time. The differences in your balance as the years pass are truly eye-opening!

Growth of $50,000 (7% average annual rate of return)

	Managed Fund (1.0% expense ratio)	Index Fund (.03% expense ratio)	Difference
10 years	$89,542	$98,082	$8,540
20 years	$160,357	$192,402	$32,045
30 years	$287,175	$377,424	$90,250
40 years	$514,286	$740,372	$226,086

Go Green

One notable constraint with many brokerage firms and advisors is their tendency to default towards investing in traditional, established companies. This approach often overlooks factors like environmental impact and employee treatment. Imagine shifting this default towards investing in businesses that lead in positive climate change policies and equitable practices.

I invite you to embrace a greener approach – to weigh the sustainability impact of your investments. Wondering where to start? Let's delve into finding and choosing green investment options that align with your values and the well-being of our planet.

Beware of Greenwashing

Greenwashing is a deceptive practice used by some companies to falsely portray their products, services, or overall brand as environmentally friendly or sustainable. Essentially, it involves marketing efforts that aim to capitalize on the growing demand for environmentally responsible products, but without the company making significant efforts to reduce its environmental impact.

In your quest for investments that are kind to the planet, you'll commonly encounter three terms: Green, Sustainable, and ESG (Environmental, Social, and Governance) Investments. While these terms are often used interchangeably, they each have distinct nuances. Think of them as branches of a tree, with ESG representing the broadest and most encompassing limb. This framework integrates a wide range of responsible practices, while the other terms focus on more specific aspects of sustainability and environmental stewardship. By understanding the subtle differences under each term, you can better align your investments with your personal values and goals for planetary well-being.

Green - companies or funds that directly contribute to environmental sustainability, such as renewable energy, pollution reduction, or conservation projects.

Sustainable - considers how a company manages its relationships with employees, suppliers, customers, and communities, in addition to its environmental stewardship.

ESG Investments - a framework for analyzing companies' conscientiousness on environmental, social, and governance factors:
- how a company performs as a steward of nature
- how it manages relationships with employees, suppliers, customers, and communities
- Governance - deals with a company's leadership, executive pay, audits, internal controls, shareholder rights.

ESG Ratings

Several agencies offer comprehensive ESG ratings for companies and funds, delving deep into various factors that measure a company's performance in these crucial areas. One such prominent agency is MSCI (**msci.com**). Here's an overview of their rating system.

CCC B	BB BBB A	AA AAA
LAGGARD	**AVERAGE**	**LEADER**
A company lagging its industry based on its high exposure and failure to manage significant ESG risks	A company with a mixed or unexceptional track record of managing the most significant ESG risks and opportunities relative to industry peers	A company leading its industry in managing the most significant ESG risks and opportunities

As you explore various investment options and platforms, keep an eye out for ESG ratings. These ratings are increasingly featured by investment firms, financial services companies, online brokerage platforms, and providers of mutual funds and ETFs. ESG ratings and analyses are also commonly included in investment research reports and in some company-issued reports. It's essential to prioritize independent ratings, as these provide an objective perspective and help you navigate past any potential greenwashing tactics employed by some companies.

Remember our lesson on fees? Seek out ESG index funds and ETFs – they're a smart choice for keeping costs low while aligning your investments with your values. Plus, there's a growing trend among robo-advisors to offer portfolios specifically tailored to ESG criteria, which can be a convenient and cost-effective way to build a portfolio that not only aims for financial returns but also considers environmental and social impact.

Give Green Bonds a Try

Green Bonds are designed to fund projects with positive environmental benefits. Issued by governments, corporations, or financial institutions, the proceeds from these bonds are earmarked for projects like renewable energy development, energy efficiency improvements, sustainable transportation, and pollution prevention.

What makes green bonds stand out in the financial landscape is their focused purpose. By investing in them, you're directly fueling projects that contribute to environmental sustainability. They're like planting seeds that grow into greener, cleaner technologies and practices.

You can purchase green bonds through most brokerage and robo-advisor platforms, offering a convenient and accessible way to add these eco-friendly investments to your portfolio. Alternatively, if you prefer a more hands-on approach, you can conduct your own independent research. Whether you choose a guided platform or go the independent route, investing in green bonds is a proactive step towards supporting environmentally beneficial projects while diversifying your investment portfolio.

The investment landscape is evolving swiftly, and with it comes a wealth of opportunities, especially in the realm of sustainable investing. We find ourselves at a pivotal point in history, where the urgency to prioritize our planet cannot be overstated. As we look ahead, here's what you should keep an eye on for future investment opportunities that go beyond traditional stocks and bonds:

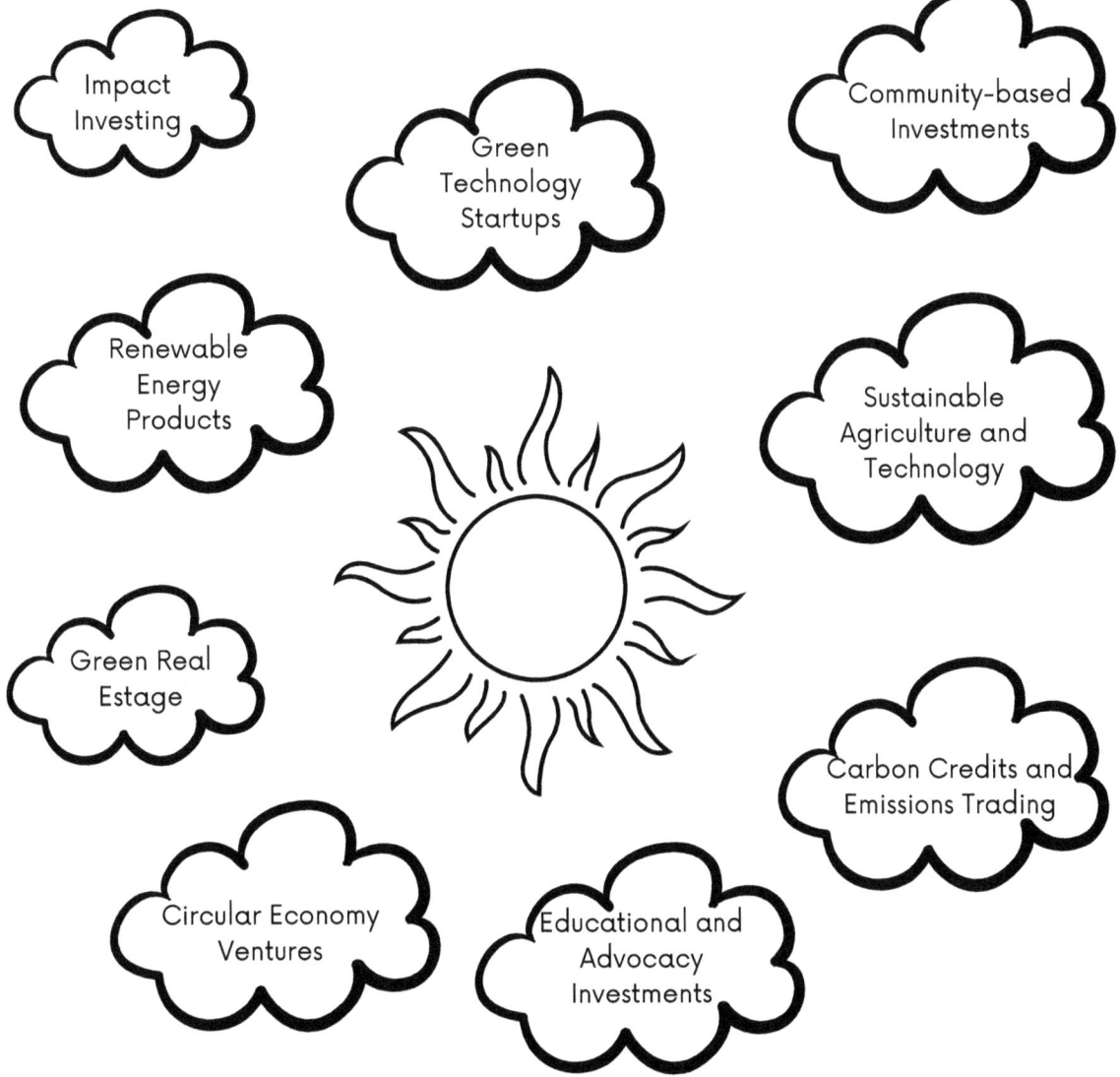

Impact Investing

Green Technology Startups

Community-based Investments

Renewable Energy Products

Sustainable Agriculture and Technology

Green Real Estage

Carbon Credits and Emissions Trading

Circular Economy Ventures

Educational and Advocacy Investments

"The future of humanity and indeed, all life on earth, now depends on us."
- Sir David Attenborough

AWESOME!

Fantastic work diving into how investing serves as your bridge to financial freedom! The key takeaway from this chapter? Those enlightening tables illustrating how annual returns and fees dramatically shape your wealth-building journey. Embrace calculated risks and remember, you're fully capable of navigating this path on your own.

☐   You learned the relationship between timeframe and investment choices.

All investments carry risk, but you can mitigate it by strategically tailoring your investments for short-term, mid-term, and long-term goals. Grasping the subtleties of each investment horizon is crucial for a balanced approach to risk and reward. Kudos to you for thoughtfully assessing your risk tolerance!

☐   You built a portfolio for your security, dream, and retirement funds.

Navigating the intricate world of investing, with its complex tax codes and various retirement plans, can be daunting, but you've managed it brilliantly! You've wisely kept your security funds in accessible savings and CDs, embraced a bit more risk with your Dream Funds, and adopted a bolder approach with your retirement funds, tailored to your timeline. And now, the $100,000 challenge awaits! Are you ready to take it on and astonish yourself? I believe in you – you've got this!

☐   You have the know-how to open an investment account and seek out environmentally friendly funds.

No room for complacency here – you're all about action! With a complete toolkit for researching, selecting, opening, funding, and managing an investment account, you're set for success. Plus, you've mastered the art of identifying opportunities that not only build wealth but also contribute to planetary sustainability. Go you!

Notes

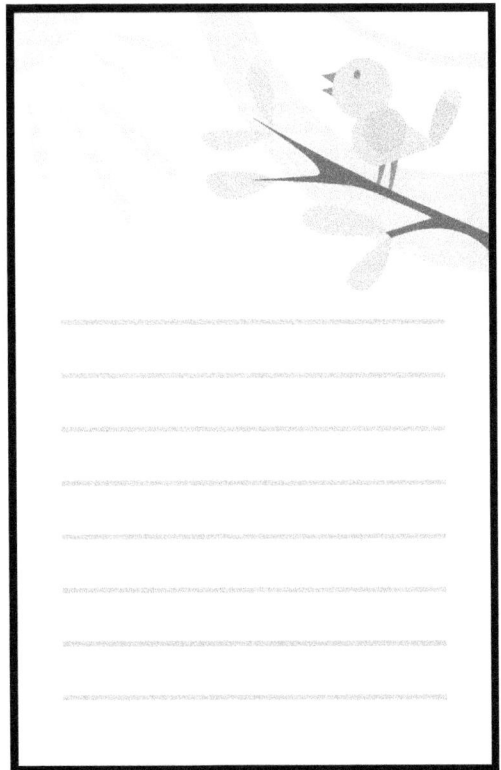

SHIFT INTO AUTOPILOT

Shift into Autopilot

You're nearing the finish line! With the Investment Bridge behind you, a smooth journey to financial freedom awaits. Ready to switch to autopilot? This is where the journey gets really fun! Stay alert and focused, as you set your finances to effectively work for themselves.

Objectives

- To explore different approaches to budgeting
- To put your finances on autopilot
- To have FUN on your journey!

Big Mission

Our mission is to give you tools and tricks that will automate your journey to financial freedom.

To-do Checklist

☐ Build a budget that works for you

☐ Use behavioral finance tricks

☐ Make a money date with yourself

☐ Have fun on your trip!

Got a Budget?

If you're keen to shift your financial journey to autopilot for the remainder, you certainly can. However, remember, much like in driving, you need to be ready to take control when the road gets rough. You've already laid solid groundwork in Chapter 5 by exploring ways to widen the gap between income and expenses. Let's build on that momentum and dive deeper into budgeting.

Budgets have Superpowers

What's the biggest obstacle on your road trip to financial freedom? Complacency. Imagine cruising along, but instead of noticing the looming thunderclouds or the sea of red taillights ahead, you tune them out. You could be headed for a financial disaster. Perhaps tackling these challenges seems overwhelming, or the myriad of potential hazards stirs up anxiety about which direction to take. Fear not – a well-crafted budget is your steadfast navigator, guiding you through every twist and turn, no matter how tough the journey gets.

Your budget wields remarkable superpowers. Consider this: your budget is a mirror of your values and priorities, a true embodiment of your identity and aspirations. It gives you a crystal-clear understanding of what you can and cannot afford, endowing you with the formidable power of **Decision Making**. With your budget, you're able to peer into the future, knowing where your money is headed not just next month, but well into the next year. This is your superpower of **Fortune Telling**.

In the face of life's surprises, your budget arms you with readiness; doom and gloom predictions can't shake you. You're endowed with the superpower of **Perseverance**. With an eye always on the big picture and an ability to adapt to changing circumstances, you've harnessed the superpower of **Perspective**.

And above all, your budget places you firmly at the helm of your financial ship. You're not just managing your money; you're commanding it, charting your own course towards your destiny. This is the superpower of **Courage**. Yes, all these extraordinary abilities spring from the simple, yet powerful act of budgeting.

Decision Making   **Fortune Telling**   **Perseverance**   **Perspective**   **Courage**

It's Time to Put on your Cape!

Given the superpowers of budgeting, you'd think there'd be a huge crowd eager to jump on the budget bandwagon. Sadly, that's rarely the case. There's a small tribe of budgeting enthusiasts, but they're pretty rare. For most folks, the word "budget" is like a signal to make a dash for the nearest exit.

Why the complicated feelings? Well, it's a mix of our individual money personalities and the dreary picture painted about budgeting – you know, the whole 'grown-up, boring task' spiel. But here's a little secret: Most of what you've been told about budgeting is wrong! It's been portrayed as a joyless chore, designed to help you control your spending. It's about discipline and deprivation. Well, who wants to sign up for that? Let's give budgeting a fresh, new spin.

OLD WAY: Your budget is a Spending Tool. It's all about discipline and sticking to set limits in each category, like groceries or entertainment. A budget can feel like a diet, where you're constantly curbing spending to stay within these self-imposed boundaries. In this scenario, savings are often an afterthought, only considered with whatever funds remain after spending.

Income - Expenses = Savings

NEW WAY: Your budget is a Savings Tool. Instead of tracking every penny you spend, your focus is on consistently diverting a part of your income into savings and investments. Budgeting is an empowering part of your financial journey, where the true satisfaction comes from seeing your net worth grow. In this model, the equation flips: your spending is determined by what's left after you've met your savings goals.

Income - Savings = Expenses

"The best budgeting tool is the one that you use."
- Brenda Uekert

Maybe you've given budgeting a shot in the past, and it just didn't click, or perhaps this is your first dive into the world of budgeting, and you're feeling a bit lost. Well, here's the secret to finding the perfect budgeting approach for you: it's a combination of understanding your money personality and choosing the tools that resonate with you. If you're a Voyager, you might love digging through the details of your budget. But if you're a Globetrotter, there's nothing fun about budgeting. Let's delve into budgeting personas and the tools that suit them best.

What type of budgeter are you? Place an 'X' in the circle next to the budgeting approach that suits you best.

O GEEK: I love spreadsheets!

O SEEKER: Give me the best budgeting software, and I'm all yours.

O APP QUEEN: If there's an easy app for it, I'll give it a whirl.

O OBJECTOR: I detest the entire budgeting process . . . must I?

Hands On or Hands Off?

How streamlined do you want your budgeting process to be? Each budgeting approach comes with its own set of advantages and disadvantages. If you opt for the "hands-on" method, where you meticulously track your expenses on a spreadsheet, you'll gain a high level of control over your spending, but not everyone enjoys the world of spreadsheets and data entry. On the other hand, the "hands-off" approach is user-friendly and convenient, but it may reduce your active involvement, potentially making it harder to maintain discipline in the long run. The biggest pitfall? Getting overwhelmed by the plethora of choices and ending up on the sidelines while your spending goes unchecked.

Indeed, the world of budgeting offers a multitude of options, and you may already have a favorite method in use. Feel free to stick with what you know. Additionally, many budgeting tools are either free or offer trial periods for experimentation. I'll guide you through various budgeting methods and suggest one or two to try. If one doesn't resonate with you, no worries—try something else.

On the following page, you'll discover the standard budget template. You can fill in your information directly or use it as a foundation to craft your personalized budget.

Monthly Budget Tracker (sample)

Income

Starting Balance	
Income Stream 1	
Income Stream 2	
Income Stream 3	
Total Income	

Food

Groceries	
Snacks and Treats	
Delivery and Takeout	
Restaurants	
Total Expenses	

Bills

Rent	
Electricity	
Water and Sewage	
Internet	
Phone	
Category 6	
Category 7	
Category 8	
Category 9	
Category 10	
Category 11	
Category 12	
Total Expenses	

Expenses

Household Items	
Household Repairs	
Apparel	
Gifts	
Fun	
Travel	
Category 7	
Category 8	
Category 9	
Category 10	
Category 11	
Category 12	
Total Expenses	

Debt

Mortgage	
Loan 1	
Loan 2	
Credit Cards	
Total Debt	

Savings

Emergency Savings	
Security Fund	
Investments	
Retirement Funds	
Total Savings	

Total

Total Income	
Total Expenses	
Total Debt	
Total Savings	
Ending Balance	

What Kind of Spender are You?

Are you all set to dive into crafting your budget? Hold up! Before we delve into the tools, let's figure out one crucial detail: your spot on the spending spectrum. Take a moment to identify which of these descriptions resonates with you the most and check the box that best fits your spending style.

☐ **Penny Pincher:** You squeeze a dollar till it hollers! Budgeting is your middle name, and you've never met a discount you didn't like.

☐ **Casual Spender**: You're comfortable spending but not overboard. For you, it's all about the occasional treat balanced with sensible budgeting.

☐ **Splurge Surfer**: Riding the waves of spending highs and lows. Some months you're all about saving, and others, you're all about spending.

☐ **Free Spirit Shopper**: You live in the moment, and your spending reflects that. You're all about enjoying life's pleasures, one purchase at a time.

Shifting into autopilot can be great, but what if unchecked spending is your default mode? For those who love shopping but find it derails their financial goals, it's time for a strategy shift. The right budgeting tool can be a game-changer for you, but it needs to be fine-tuned to curb your enthusiastic spending.

Time to play financial detective. Head on back to your Wants versus Needs tracker. Where is your money really going? Whether it's frequent restaurant visits, online shopping sprees, or spontaneous gadget buys, identifying these patterns is key to regaining control of your finances.

After you've mapped out where your money is going, it's action time. Review the following list of potential changes and mark the ones you're ready to commit to. This is about making conscious choices to spend smarter, not just less.

☐ Designate your Shopping Days

Designate one or two days each month as your exclusive shopping days. Feel free to add items to your online cart throughout the month, giving you time to consider and prioritize what you really need or want. Resist the urge to click 'Buy Now.' By transforming shopping into a special event rather than a daily habit, you bring more mindfulness and control into your spending.

Use cash or store cards with a set amount

If your splurges are local, you can get a set amount of cash out each month and pay in cash. Or use store cards with a set amount - a strategy that can also work for online purchases.

Create a 'Fun Fund'

Turn shopping into an occasion, not a routine activity. Create a 'Fun Fund' - a designated account for discretionary spending. By setting up a special fund with a predetermined limit, you can indulge in your favorite pastimes guilt-free.

Remember, this journey is about balance – enjoying the present while smoothly sailing towards a future of financial security. Embrace this new phase of budgeting with confidence and watch as your financial autopilot steers you towards success. Now let's talk about budgeting approaches.

Geek out on Spreadsheets!

If personal finance is your playground and spreadsheets are your go-to (shoutout to the engineers and tech gurus!), then budgeting can be as thrilling as cracking a complex code. It's no surprise that many early retirees from tech and engineering fields excel in financial planning. Their typically robust salaries, combined with a love for data analysis, position them perfectly as budgeting pros. The real charm of spreadsheets? Their unmatched flexibility and control. You can fine-tune your budget with the precision of a programmer, adjusting it to fit your life's weekly ebbs and flows.

Looking back at my own financial path, I discovered that blending different methods hit the sweet spot. My MVP? A straightforward electronic checkbook register. This humble tool, along with my approach of saving and investing at least half of my income, was pivotal in achieving financial freedom. This strategy is a winner, particularly honing your fortune-telling skills.

Since you're on the geekier side of the spectrum, scouting out Excel or Google Sheets budget templates will be a walk in the park for you. And if you're curious about the checkbook register that was a game-changer for me, it's just a click away at **bit.ly/checkbookregister**. Dive in and watch those numbers work their magic!

Software for Seekers

The software world is brimming with budgeting tools, and as a seeker of the best, you're in for a treat. Many come with free versions, offering basic features with the option to upgrade for additional functionalities. For those ready to invest a bit more, paid versions frequently provide a free trial period, allowing you to test the waters before committing. Doing your research is key, including seeking out independent reviews to get unbiased opinions.

Year after year, You Need a Budget (YNAB) stands out as a top contender in the realm of budgeting software (check it out at **ynab.com**). It may not be everyone's cup of tea, but it's definitely worth a test drive. YNAB offers a unique approach to managing finances that could be just the tool you're looking for to streamline your budgeting process.

Options for App Queens

The digital realm is a treasure trove of online budgeting tools, each tailored to meet various financial needs and preferences. Why not explore what's already in your pocket? Your bank's app might have a built-in budgeting feature. Other popular choices include Mint and PocketGuard, known for their user-friendly interfaces. And for those who like a bit of fun with their finances, there are apps that gamify budgeting, turning the act of saving money into an engaging game. Your mission is to find an app that resonates with you, whether you're after simplicity, comprehensive analysis, or a playful approach to managing money.

Diving into these apps is a breeze – just download and start exploring. Take a week or two to test each app, seeing how well it meshes with your financial habits and needs. Keep an eye on how it categorizes your spending, the effectiveness of its alerts, and how seamlessly it integrates with your accounts. The ease of use is crucial, too – some apps are intuitive right off the bat, while others might take a bit more time to get the hang of. The ideal app for you is the one that not only streamlines your financial management but also adds an element of fun to the process.

The Anti-Budget for Objectors

If the very thought of budgeting makes you cringe, don't worry, you're not alone. For those who can't stand the idea of tracking every penny, there's a refreshing alternative known as the anti-budget (made popular by financial blogger, Paula Pant). The anti-budget is for those who want financial control without the nitty-gritty of traditional budgeting.

The anti-budget is beautifully simple. Instead of meticulously categorizing your expenses, you start by saving a significant portion of your income right off the bat, depending on your financial goals. This money goes straight into your savings or investment accounts. What's left is yours to spend without guilt or complex tracking. The key here is to ensure that your essential expenses (rent, bills, debt payments) are covered, leaving the rest for discretionary spending. This method turns the traditional budgeting approach on its head – you save first and then live on the rest, offering a liberating take on managing your money. It's ideal for those who want to maintain financial health without getting bogged down by every little detail.

So, which budgeting style will you choose? Tick the box next to the approach that seems like the best fit for you. And remember, it's all about experimentation – you can try different methods until you find the one that clicks perfectly with your money personality and budgeting style.

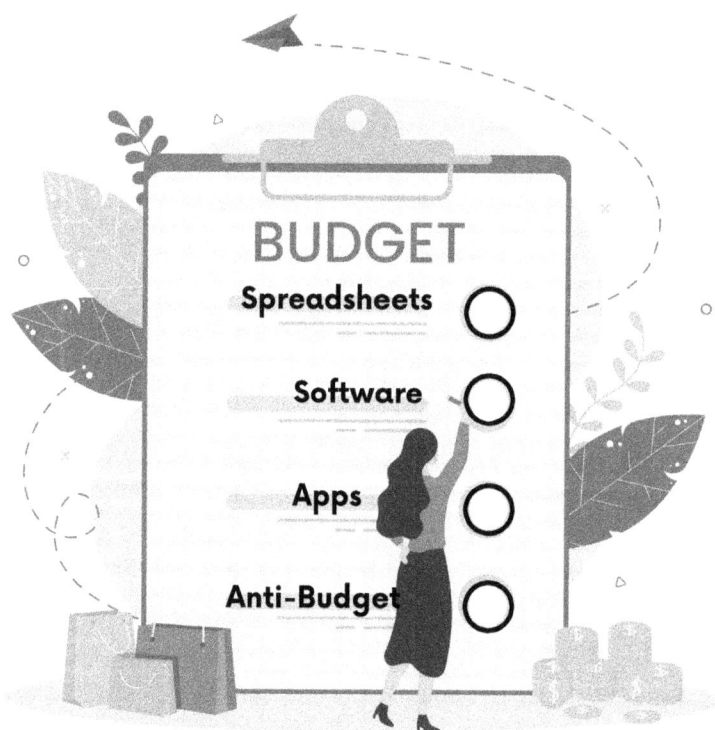

You've made fantastic progress with your budgeting! Now, how about a little inspiration? Dive into this story about three friends and their budgeting journeys. It's a tale that will not only motivate you but also reassure you that whichever approach you choose, it's bound to be effective as long as you put it into practice. Let their experiences show you the diverse paths to success!

A Tale of Three Friends

In the bustling heart of the city, nestled among quaint bookstores and vibrant murals, sits a cozy coffee shop, Café Serendipity. It's here, under the warm glow of the lights, that three friends – Amara, Leo, and Sam – gather for their monthly coffee ritual.

Amara has always had a knack for numbers. Her approach to budgeting is as meticulous as it is effective. With an array of spreadsheets, she meticulously tracks every expenditure and saving. Amara's eyes light up as she explains how her spreadsheets help prioritize her savings, aligning each dollar with her future goals. Her friends often tease her about her spreadsheet obsession, but they can't help but admire her dedication.

Then there's Leo, an easy-going guy with a zest for life, who used to view budgeting as a buzzkill. He confesses how he once despised the very idea of tracking expenses, often finding himself in a tangle of overspending. But recently, he's taken a leap into the world of the anti-budget. "It's liberating!" he exclaims, describing how setting aside savings first and then freely spending the rest has transformed his financial habits. His newfound approach has brought a balance of responsibility and spontaneity to his life.

Sam brings a tech-savvy flair to the group. They've turned budgeting into a game, using an app that rewards them for meeting savings goals and staying under budget. "It's like playing a financial video game," Sam explains with a grin, "except the points I score are real dollars in my bank account!" Their enthusiasm for gamified budgeting is infectious, and it's clear they've found a method that resonates with their playful yet goal-oriented nature.

As they sip their lattes and share laughs, the trio reflects on their diverse budgeting styles. What's evident is that despite their different approaches, each has found a way to make budgeting work for them, proving that there's no one-size-fits-all solution to managing money. In this little coffee shop, Amara, Leo, and Sam celebrate their individual successes, each journey as unique as the flavors in their cups.

-DONT- STAND IN your OWN WAY

Secret Autopilot Tips

Now that you've set your budget, it's time to smooth out the rest of your financial journey with the development of smart habits. You see, the key to effortless financial management lies in understanding and tweaking our behavior. Enter the fascinating world of behavioral finance – a field that delves deep into our financial behaviors and how we can adjust them for the better. This realm of study is chock-full of insightful tips and strategies designed to keep your finances on autopilot, effortlessly steering you towards your goals.

Behavioral finance isn't just about numbers and charts; it's about understanding why we make the financial decisions we do and how to harness this knowledge for our benefit. From identifying triggers that lead to impulsive spending to setting up systems that automate savings, these insights help transform your financial habits from obstacles to allies. By applying these principles, you can reinforce positive financial behaviors, making smart money management second nature. Think of it as fine-tuning your financial engine so that you cruise towards success with ease and confidence.

Behavioral finance is a vast and varied field, but we'll hone in on three key aspects that are particularly relevant: herd behavior, mental accounting, and timing. Let's dive into a brief overview of each to understand how they impact our financial decisions.

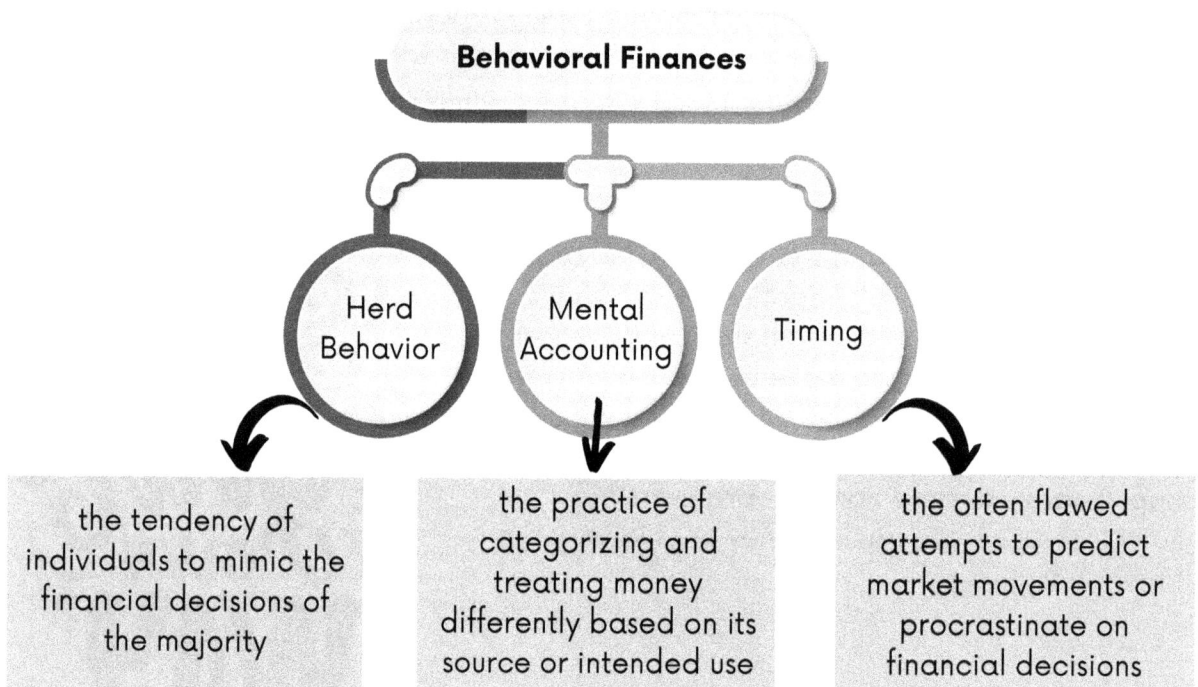

Behavioral Finances

Herd Behavior — the tendency of individuals to mimic the financial decisions of the majority

Mental Accounting — the practice of categorizing and treating money differently based on its source or intended use

Timing — the often flawed attempts to predict market movements or procrastinate on financial decisions

Tip 1: Take the road less traveled

On our financial road trip, there's one detour you'll want to avoid: the Herd Highway. It's easy to get swept up in the excitement when everyone is rushing to buy houses or stocks, thinking, "If everyone's doing it, it must be right!" But here's the twist: when the whole crowd is heading one way, it's often wisest to take a different route.

For example, look at the housing bubble burst in 2008. Everyone was buying real estate, prices skyrocketed, and then – pop! Those who followed the herd found themselves in a financial jam. The same goes for other investments, like stocks, gold, and cryptocurrency; when everyone's buying, prices inflate, creating a bubble that can burst. So, on your Money Road Trip, keep a cool head. When you see a herd stampeding towards the latest 'hot' investment, it might be your cue to hit the brakes, pull out your map, and find your own path. Remember, the road less traveled often leads to the most scenic – and financially sound – destinations.

☐ Stick to your plan. Don't jump into things due to FOMO (the fear of missing out).

☐ Stay diversified, so that one bad investment doesn't ruin your financial life.

"Be fearful when others are greedy, and be greedy when others are fearful."
- Warren Buffet

Tip 2: Check your friends at the door

The saying "you're the average of the five people you spend the most time with" rings particularly true in the realm of finances. It's fascinating how much our social circle can sway our spending habits, savings behaviors, and investment choices. For example, if your friends are avid stock market investors, there's a good chance you'll find yourself drawn to investing as well. Similarly, if your buddies have a penchant for splurging on antique shopping, don't be surprised if you start developing a similar spending habit.

This doesn't mean you need to overhaul your friend group, but it does suggest the importance of being mindful of the influence your peers have on your financial decisions. If your social life often revolves around expensive nights out, high-end shopping sprees, or lavish vacations, it might be time to consider alternatives that won't strain your budget. If your current circle isn't supportive of your financial goals, it might be time to seek out new connections.

☐ Suggest alternatives to expensive outings, like game night or exploring local parks and community events.

☐ Set a limit on how much you will spend on "friends' events."

☐ Join groups and connect with people who are more in tune with your values and goals.

Use Mental Accounting Tricks

Tip 3: Use "found money" to accelerate your goals

Picture this: You're walking past an ATM and, lo and behold, you find $50 hidden in the bushes. There's no one around, so you pick it up. Suddenly, you're on cloud nine with this unexpected windfall! The thought of a lavish dinner with a glass of wine crosses your mind, deviating from your usual sensible dinner plan. Why not? It's free money, right?

This scenario taps into a common human instinct. When we come across "found money" – like bonuses, tax refunds, or unexpected inheritances – we often treat it differently from our hard-earned income. There's a tendency to splurge on luxuries or experiences we wouldn't usually consider with our regular paycheck. It's easy to mentally earmark this surprise cash for something indulgent, like the latest tech gadget or a dream vacation, even when pressing financial responsibilities like debt or a scant emergency fund loom in the background.

Yes, it's fantastic to have this surprise cash in hand, and the urge to enjoy it is natural. But remember, without mindful planning, today's "found money" can quickly become tomorrow's "vanished funds." So, while it's perfectly fine to treat yourself a bit, consider also how this unexpected bonus can bolster your financial security and future goals.

☐ Treat "found money" like regular income. Use it to fund your priorities.

☐ Have fun with some of it! It's okay to take a small portion of your "found money" and use it for a splurge.

Tip 4: Adapt your budget as circumstances change

Since you've successfully navigated through our comprehensive section on budgeting, you're brimming with discipline and determination. But let's face it, life is full of surprises and shifts. So, what do you do when life takes an unexpected turn, or when your priorities evolve?

Let's consider a relatable example: Jamie, a graphic designer. In January, she sets a budget with allocations for rent, utilities, food, entertainment, and a modest sum for travel. Mid-year, Jamie gets a freelance project that boosts her income significantly. Instead of letting this extra cash flow into random spending, she adapts her budget. She increases her savings rate, allocates more for professional development courses, and plans a slightly more lavish vacation.

Then, as the year progresses, Jamie encounters an unexpected expense: her laptop needs a costly repair. She revisits her budget again, temporarily reducing her entertainment and travel allocations to cover the cost. Once the laptop is fixed and she's back on track, she readjusts her spending to resume her original plans.

This flexibility is the essence of adaptable budgeting. It's not about scrapping your budget at the first sign of change, but rather tweaking it to accommodate new developments - be they positive (like increased income) or challenging (like unforeseen expenses). By doing so, Jamie not only manages to stay within her overall financial boundaries but also ensures that her budget continually aligns with her evolving needs and goals.

- [ ] Keep your budget categories flexible; they're just guidelines. Consider the fluidity of the anti-budget approach.

- [ ] Tap into your emergency fund for unforeseen expenses and remember to refill it to maintain your financial safety net.

"Money looks better in the bank than on your feet."
- Sophia Amoruso

Tip 5: Round up to gain an advantage

How often have you been at a checkout counter and heard the cashier ask if you'd like to "round up" your total to the nearest dollar for charity? You might think, "Sure, why not? It's only a bit of spare change." Now imagine if you redirected this 'round-up' strategy towards your own savings. Think about how all those bits of 'loose change' can accumulate significantly over a multitude of transactions. This approach can be a subtle, yet powerful, way to enhance your personal wealth.

For example, when it comes to your car loan, you might casually say your monthly payment is "around $700," though it could actually be $677.58.   By rounding up to a neat $700 and directing the extra $22.42 towards your loan's principal, you can effectively shorten the loan duration and save on interest. Similarly, consider the power of rounding up for everyday purchases - there are apps that will do this automatically. Buy a coffee for $3.76, and the app rounds it to $4, funneling that $0.24 difference into savings. Over time, these small contributions can add up to a substantial amount.

This rounding-up method is more than just a savings tool; it's a mindset shift. It cultivates the habit of consistently earmarking small amounts for savings, fostering a more disciplined financial approach. As you observe your 'round-up' savings grow, it not only brings the satisfaction of watching your wealth increase but also offers insights into your spending habits. It transforms everyday spending into a proactive saving adventure, perfectly aligning with the goal of building wealth in a smart, seamless manner.

- [ ] Round up your loan payments to the nearest $100 (or $1,000 if you're ambitious), with the "extra" applied to the principal.

- [ ] Use a FREE app that will automatically round up your purchases and move the "excess" into a savings account. (Search for apps that round up your purchases.)

Timing is Everything!

Tip 6: Automate!

Ready to turbocharge your wealth-building journey with a bit of financial cruise control? Enter the world of automation! It's like setting your finances on autopilot, perfectly aligned with our human tendency to, well, sometimes drag our feet. Let's face it – we all have those moments where we plan to do something important (like saving for the future), but then life happens, and suddenly it's next month, then next year, and we're still at the starting line.

This is where automating your savings and investments comes in as a game-changer. Think of it as your financial co-pilot. By setting up automatic transfers to your savings account, retirement fund, or investment portfolio, you're bypassing the procrastination station. And here's a fun twist: many retirement accounts now use an 'opt-out' approach. This means you're automatically on the saving track, but here's a pro tip: crank up that default saving rate to turbo-boost your journey to financial freedom.

In short, automating your finances is like having a smart, savvy friend who makes sure you're always moving forward on your road trip, even when you're busy enjoying the scenery. It keeps your financial engine running smoothly towards your goals, so you can relax and enjoy the ride. And the best part? You'll be amazed at how your wealth grows over time, almost like magic, but it's just smart financial planning!

- [ ] Automate payments for major bills, like mortgage and loan payments. Strive to automate your credit card payments, ensuring you pay off the full balance each month.

- [ ] Automate deposits into your savings accounts, investment accounts, and retirement accounts.

183

Tip 7: Invest through good and bad times

Navigating the investment landscape can sometimes lead to overconfidence, especially when luck smiles on us early in the game. Imagine snapping up a stock at a bargain and watching it skyrocket overnight. You're feeling like a financial whiz, and naturally, you want to share this success with your friends. But then, as quickly as fortunes rose, they can plummet – maybe that hot company goes belly-up, or the CEO of your favorite crypto coin vanishes with the funds. This is a classic case of overconfidence, luring us into believing we can outsmart the market, buying low and selling high – a feat easier said than done.

This is where Dollar-Cost Averaging (DCA) comes to the rescue, steering us away from the tricky path of market timing. DCA is not about making a big splash with a single investment; it's about consistent, regular investments over time, regardless of market ups and downs. Think of it as your reliable financial GPS guiding you through the twists and turns of investing.

Here's how it works. Let's say you decide to invest $100 every month into an index fund. Some months, when the market is down, your $100 buys more shares because they're cheaper. And when the market is up, the same amount buys fewer shares. It's like shopping for deals – sometimes you get more bang for your buck! Over the long haul, this strategy evens out your investment cost. No more fretting about the "perfect" time to invest, because you're smoothing out the risks across the calendar. What's more, it strips away the emotional rollercoaster of investing – you're playing a steady, consistent game, not chasing market highs and lows.

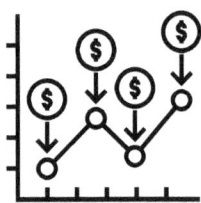

☐ Investigate high-quality, ESG-labeled investments that you're confident in holding for years to come.

☐ Ignore the doom-and-gloom claims that often lead to panic selling. Stay focused on your long-term financial strategy.

> **"Time is your friend; impulse is your enemy. Take advantage of compound interest and don't be captivated by the siren song of the market"**
> **- John Bogle**

Tip 8: Leverage milestones

Recall those mile markers dotting the route of our journey to financial freedom? Personal milestones, much like those markers, can serve as crucial guideposts in our financial voyage. But here's a fun twist: instead of mere time markers, these milestones are sparkling opportunities to accelerate your financial growth and success. Take the new year, for instance. It's not just a time for resolutions and fireworks; it's 365 (or 366) blank pages waiting to be filled with your financial triumphs. What goals do you want to achieve in this fresh chapter? How will you make this year count financially?

Then come those big milestone birthdays and life-changing events – each a golden opportunity to reassess and reenergize your financial strategy. Think of them not just as years added, but as wisdom gained, especially in the realm of finance. Hitting 30, 40, or 50 isn't just about getting older; it's about getting wiser – financially wiser, that is. These aren't just numbers; they're like checkpoints on your financial roadmap. They're moments to pull over, check your wealth fuel gauge, and maybe even recalibrate your route. Ask yourself critical questions: Are you saving enough for those golden years? Is it time to diversify your investments or start planning for a child's education?

And it's not just about age-related milestones. Landing a new job, celebrating a work anniversary, or even paying off a big loan – each of these events is a chance to reassess and readjust your financial strategy. Maybe it's time to increase your security fund, or perhaps you're ready to venture into new investment territories. In essence, every personal milestone is an opportunity to ensure your journey towards financial freedom is not just on track but also tailored to your evolving life stages.

☐ Each new year, set a financial goal and craft an action plan detailing specific steps to achieve it.

☐ Visualize where you want to be by your next milestone birthday, both personally and financially. Place an inspiring image or quote on your refrigerator as a daily reminder.

Tip 9: Embrace purchase procrastination

In our fast-paced world, spending money, especially with a credit card, can be almost too easy. The real pinch of the cost doesn't hit until the bill rolls in. But let's talk about those times when our spending isn't just about needs or wants, but more about responding to emotions – hello, retail therapy! You know the drill: a tough day leads to a tub of your favorite ice cream, and before you know it, you're online, clicking away on the latest fashion or that life-changing book.

Ready for a gear shift? Let's swap that impulsive retail therapy for a more mindful spending approach. Imagine putting a pause on those 'buy-now' impulses, transforming them into 'let's-think-about-it' moments. The key is to introduce a bit of healthy procrastination into our buying habits. When you feel the urge to make a purchase, especially if it's driven by emotions, pause. Give yourself a day or two to mull over the purchase. Often, you'll find that the desire to buy fades, or you realize that the item isn't as essential as it seemed in the heat of the moment.

This approach isn't about denying yourself joy or comfort; it's about ensuring your spending is intentional and truly beneficial. It's about disconnecting the automatic link between emotions and spending. Instead of seeking comfort in shopping, explore other, more fulfilling ways to address your mood. Perhaps a walk, a chat with a friend, or indulging in a hobby could be the answer. By practicing mindful spending, you're not just saving money; you're also cultivating a healthier, more conscious approach to your finances, where each purchase is a deliberate choice, not a reflex.

☐ Practice the 24-Hour Cart Pause. Let items linger in your online cart for at least a day, then re-evaluate.

☐ Designate mindful spending days for all your household and personal shopping needs.

Tip 10: Make a money date with yourself

We saved the best tip for last - set up a 'Money Date' with yourself! It's like a refreshing pit stop on your financial journey, a dedicated moment each week to tune up your fiscal engine. Pick a day – be it Money Monday, Finance Friday, or Savings Saturday – and mark it in your calendar. This is your special time to review, update, and strategize your finances. Think of it as a rendezvous with your budget and goals, ensuring everything's running smoothly on your road to financial freedom.

Imagine this: It's Finance Friday, your chosen day. You grab your favorite beverage, find a comfy spot, and it's just you and your finances. No distractions, no rush. You review your budget, track your spending, and maybe even learn something new about investing or saving. It's your time to celebrate your financial wins, like sticking to your budget, and strategize over any bumps you hit during the week.

So, circle a day on your calendar, and make it a recurring event. This regular check-in keeps your financial goals on track and ensures you're always steering in the right direction. Plus, it's a great way to make managing your money an enjoyable and rewarding part of your week. Let's turn financial management into a date you look forward to, filled with insights, progress, and a bit of fun!

☐ Schedule a weekly 'Financial Check-in' in your calendar, complete with a reminder. Commit to show up!

☐ Treat yourself to a small reward after successfully completing a month of your scheduled 'Money Dates

My money dates will be on (circle one)

Sunday   Monday   Tuesday   Wednesday   Thursday   Friday   Saturday

at (time) _____ am / pm

NEVER Stop growing

Abby Charts her Course to Financial Freedom

Abby's story began on a path many find themselves on – weighed down by credit card debt and the burden of emotional shopping. Each swipe of her card was a temporary escape from a job that drained her spirit and a life that seemed to be veering off course. Her shopping sprees were her solace, but they left her with a growing mountain of debt and a sinking feeling of despair.

But Abby's story is one of metamorphosis and empowerment. On a day that felt like any other, amidst the clutter of unopened bills and receipts, Abby had her moment of reckoning. She realized the key to a brighter future lay in rewriting her financial script. It began with a deep dive into her expenses and debts, an overwhelming but necessary first step towards change.

Abby's road to financial freedom was paved with strategic and mindful decisions. She embraced the anti-budget approach – a system that allowed her the flexibility to manage her finances without the confines of strict categorization, but with the discipline to prioritize savings and debt repayment. Abby found solace in simple yet effective financial tools, like apps that rounded up her purchases to the nearest dollar, slowly but steadily building her savings.

One of the most transformative changes in Abby's journey was redefining her relationship with shopping. She combated her retail therapy habit by implementing a 24-hour rule – letting potential purchases sit in her online shopping cart for a day before deciding. This pause gave Abby time to reflect on the necessity of her purchases, often leading to the realization that the joy of buying was fleeting compared to the satisfaction of financial stability.

As her 30th birthday approached, Abby visualized what she wanted her life to look like – not just financially, but personally and professionally. This vision became a guiding light, influencing her spending and saving habits. It wasn't about cutting out all the joys of life; it was about creating a balance where she could enjoy the present while building a secure future.

Abby's journey to financial freedom was more than a ledger of cleared debts or a growing savings account. It was a voyage of rediscovery, finding joy in the simple things – a coffee with friends, a beloved book, a stroll in the park. These experiences replaced the fleeting thrill of retail therapy, filling her life with genuine contentment.

In the end, Abby's journey to financial freedom was more than just reaching a set of financial goals; it was about rediscovering herself, her passions, and her aspirations. Her story is a powerful reminder of the strength within each of us to take control of our finances and, in doing so, transform our lives. As she celebrated her 30th birthday, Abby looked back not just at a journey of financial recovery, but at a journey of self-discovery and empowerment, a true testament to the resilience of the human spirit.

· You're · AMAZING

Have Fun on your Road Trip!

Let's shift gears and focus on an essential element of this journey – having fun! Yes, the road to financial freedom isn't just about numbers, budgets, and savings; it's also about embracing the joy and adventures along the way. Imagine this journey dotted with spontaneous detours, laughter-filled pit stops, and unexpected, delightful roadside attractions. These moments of fun are not just breaks in the journey; they're integral parts of the trip that make the whole experience richer and more memorable.

Picture your financial journey as a scenic road trip. Along the way, there are incredible views, quirky roadside stands, and hidden gems that you stumble upon – these are the joys of life that money can't buy, yet are funded by your financial wisdom. Set up that 'Fun Account' – a little stash dedicated solely to life's pleasures, be it a spontaneous weekend getaway, a concert of your favorite band, or a treat-yourself day. It's your financial pat on the back, a reward for staying on track.

And why make this journey alone? Turn your financial goals into a group adventure. Involve your family or friends, make it a shared experience. Set common goals and celebrate milestones together, be it paying off debt, saving for a big goal, or simply sticking to your budget for the month. Turn budget discussions with your family into fun, interactive sessions where everyone gets a say and a share in the fun budget. If you're on this road trip with friends, how about a savings challenge? Whoever hits their goal first gets treated to dinner by the others!

Most crucially, treasure each moment of this journey. Remember, the road to financial freedom is sprinkled with laughter, spontaneous detours, and those unforgettable roadside wonders Celebrate your successes, learn from the detours, and always keep an eye out for those unexpected joys. Financial freedom isn't just a destination; it's a way of traveling. It's about finding the balance between saving for tomorrow and living fully today. So, as you cruise down this road, make sure to roll down the windows, turn up the music, and enjoy the ride. After all, the best part of a road trip isn't just where you're going; it's the fun you have along the way!

> **"I am going to have fun every day I'm given on this planet."**
> **- Queen Latifah**

AWESOME!

Incredible work! With a dynamic budget in place, your financial future is gleaming brightly. I can sense you confidently cruising ahead, glancing in the rearview mirror with pride at the remarkable progress you've made. Let's hit the pause button and look back at the milestones you've crossed in this chapter, 'Shift into Autopilot.' Think of it as a scenic overlook on your financial freedom journey.

☐ You drafted a budget and found your favorite tool.

Budgeting isn't about deprivation and discipline – it's a powerful shift towards aligning your money with your priorities and relishing in its growth. Remember, you're in the driver's seat of your financial journey. And here's the fun part: exploring different budgeting tools isn't just a good idea, it's part of the adventure! There's a perfect match out there for your unique personality and preferences.

☐ You picked up some powerful tips that will keep your journey smooth.

Welcome to the vast and enlightening world of behavioral finance, brimming with insights that can revolutionize your financial journey. You've gathered a treasure trove of strategies centered around herd behavior, mental accounting, and timing. These tips are your key to smoothly shifting into autopilot and maintaining that course. And let's not forget your scheduled weekly 'Money Date' – a highlight in your calendar that you eagerly anticipate.

☐ You are on a mission to savor the journey and have fun along the way.

As you journey closer to your destination, remember, it's not just about the miles covered, but the experiences along the way. The path to financial freedom shouldn't be a monotonous drive on a never-ending freeway. It's about embracing the fun – like pulling over at quirky roadside attractions, making new friends, and embarking on spontaneous adventures. Financial freedom transcends mere numbers and calculations; it's about crafting a lifestyle that nurtures your joy and excitement. So go ahead, relish the fun moments along the way!

Notes

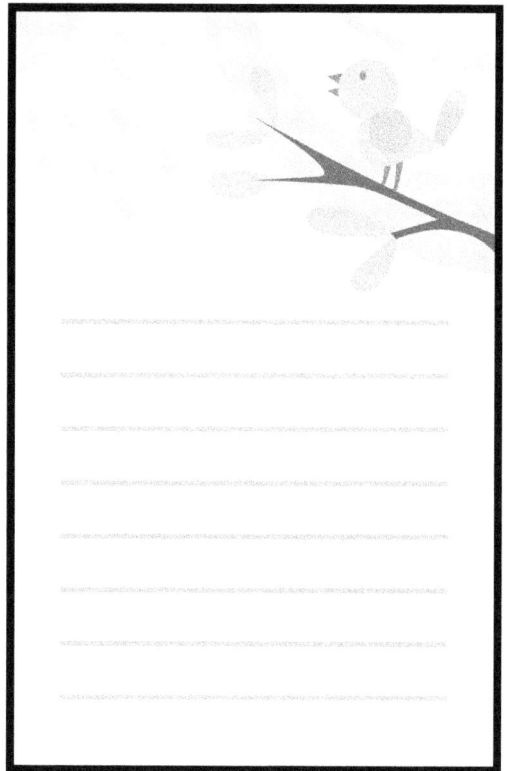

9

LOVE YOUR DESTINATION

Love your Destination

You've made it to financial freedom – congratulations! Now's the time to take bold steps and embrace this new chapter with courage. Let your hard-earned financial freedom be the key that unlocks the door to living out your dreams.

⦿ Objectives

- To explore new horizons and design your life
- To practice resilience when things don't go your way
- To build a joy-filled life

Big Mission

Our mission is to help you leverage your newfound freedom in living a life rich with purpose, joy, and fulfillment.

To-do Checklist

☐ Design your life

☐ Make an action plan

☐ Write down your "dandelion moments"

Design your Life

Hooray, you've just cruised past the finish line of financial freedom! That's a huge win, and you should definitely give yourself a pat on the back. But here's a little secret: crossing this milestone doesn't mean life does a complete 180. You might find yourself cruising onwards, tweaking your goal towards financial independence, where work becomes a choice rather than a necessity. And guess what? Now you can ease off the gas pedal a bit. It's the perfect time to start turning some of those dreams into reality!

But let's chat about something real for a moment. What if you park at your financial freedom destination and it doesn't quite match the postcard you had in your mind? Maybe the sun isn't always shining, and yes, there's still laundry waiting for you. Perhaps the dreams you had when you embarked on this journey have evolved over time. That's perfectly okay!

I'm unfolding my story for you – not just as a roadmap but as a travel buddy's diary. It's to show you that it's perfectly normal for your journey and destination to take their own unique shapes. Let this be your inspiration to adapt, grow, and find joy in this new phase of your adventure. Welcome to the next chapter of your road trip, where the real fun begins – living out your financial freedom in a way that's true to you!

Dr. Brenda Builds a Life of Adventure

My quest was for financial independence – that sweet spot where work shifts from necessity to choice. There I was, cruising at the peak of my career, with a shiny reputation and a hefty salary. But deep down, I was running on empty, burned out and questioning if this was all there was to my life. Then, one fateful day, everything changed. I hit that pivotal moment, and with a burst of clarity, I hopped off the career treadmill. It was a leap into the unknown, but oh, what a thrilling leap it was! When I walked out of my office for the last time, boxes in hand, I felt something I hadn't felt in ages – pure relief. Sure, it wasn't the exit I'd planned, but I was free, with enough savings to give me breathing space to ponder my next move.

Suddenly, Mondays transformed from mundane to marvelous – they were for hikes, leisurely errands, and moments of peace in the gazebo. The financial pressure had eased, giving me time to reflect on what I truly wanted. I knew diving back into my old field would mean moving or juggling consulting gigs. I craved a fresh start. More than anything, I wanted to empower others with the knowledge to achieve financial freedom, to ensure they wouldn't find themselves stuck in a job they didn't love. This new purpose became my driving force.

For the next 18 months, my dining room table transformed into my command center. I delved into becoming a Financial Coach and began shaping what would eventually blossom into the Financial Freedom Academy. Yet, the reality hit hard: I was clocking more hours for myself than in my previous job, and the entrepreneurial path was tougher than I'd envisioned.

I found myself in a spiral of misery. Reflecting on my past career, it wasn't just the steady paycheck I missed – I longed for the travel and the human connections. Instead, I was anchored to the same view of my suburban street, pouring my energy into a venture still waiting to take off. My health declined, my spirits sank, and I questioned my situation: What use was financial freedom if it meant confinement to my dining room table?

My home, once my sanctuary, began to feel like a weight. I contemplated a life unshackled from the house. Even though I owned it outright, it demanded upkeep – new windows, a roof, heating and cooling systems. The gardens I loved now seemed like endless chores. With my child grown and independent, the need for such a large space vanished. The thought of selling it sparked a glimmer of possibility: Could this be my chance to reinvent my life?

Then, on a crisp October day while visiting family in the Midwest, everything clicked. A detour to an RV dealership opened my eyes. Stepping into an RV, I saw my future – a life of adventure powered by financial freedom. That following May, I left my house keys on the counter for the new owners, and with a heart full of hope and excitement, I embarked on a new journey in my motorhome, ready to embrace a life defined by exploration and discovery.

My new life as an RVer was both terrifying and thrilling. It was just me and my three lovely cats, hitting the open road together. I distinctly remember that first week, camped in the tranquil embrace of the Blue Ridge Mountains, with the haunting howls of distant coyotes breaking the silence of the night. In those moments, I couldn't help but wonder, "What have I just done?" Stepping so far out of my comfort zone was daunting, yet I knew deep down this was my chance to discover my true self and a life of joy.

Those first six months were a rollercoaster of emotions, with doubt as my constant companion. Every new sound in the night, every unfamiliar path, and each unexpected challenge was a test of my resolve. Yet, with each passing day and every mile traveled, I was slowly but surely crafting a new chapter, one filled with discovery, growth, and the kind of exhilaration that comes from embracing the unknown. This journey was far more than a mere change of scenery; it was a transformative adventure that rekindled the spirit of my youth, filling me with a sense of wonder and freedom reminiscent of my earlier days.

Allow Yourself Joy

My physical, mental, and emotional health soared. Hiking in a Texas state park, I found myself smiling, a feeling that had become wonderfully familiar. I jokingly remarked to an acquaintance, "I might just wear out my smile muscles at this rate." Joy was my companion on the trails, peace my blanket under starry skies, and gratitude my emotion as I cuddled with my cats. In this journey, I hadn't just found a new lifestyle; I had discovered joy.

A few years into my adventure, I found myself in a deep conversation with my business coach, my feet in the Oregon coast's sand, watching waves crash against rocks. She asked how I transformed from an overworked professional and house-bound entrepreneur to an adventurous nomad. My reply was straightforward: "The formula is quite simple - have a dream, make a plan, save your money, and step into your life - Dream Plan Save Do." The hardest part, I shared, was the 'Do' – stepping out of your comfort zone. Embracing bravery to redesign your life can lead to unparalleled joy, a testament to the power of courage in charting new paths.

Applying Design Theory

My leap into a new lifestyle was influenced by design theory – the concept of using engineering principles to craft a life that truly resonates with me. This idea originates from a Stanford University course created by Bill Burnett and Dale Evans, which encourages you to be the architect of your destiny, employing brainstorming, prototyping, and iterative testing to discover different life and career paths. It's all about custom-building a life that sings to your rhythm, fueled by continuous experimentation and adaptation.

This groundbreaking approach didn't just change lives; it inspired a book, "Designing Your Life: How to Build a Well-Lived, Joyful Life" (Knopf, 2016). And guess what? Now that you've cruised into your own zone of financial freedom, this 'designing your life' concept is like a GPS guiding you to tailor-make your life. It's not just about going with the flow; it's about steering your ship with intention, balancing the art of living with the acts of doing, navigating life's uncertainties, and embracing a mindset geared for growth and lifelong learning.

So, let's take these cool concepts and map them onto your own journey. Think of it as customizing your road trip – choosing the routes that excite you, stopping at the spots that intrigue you, and continually learning from each twist and turn. Your financial freedom is just the start – now, you get to design the rest of the ride!

Design Concepts

1. Be curious
2. Try stuff
3. Reframe problems
4. Know it's a process
5. Ask for help

Design theory's focus on four spheres – work, play, love, and health – is akin to finding yourself at a traffic circle with four distinct exits after an exhilarating road trip. Each exit leads to a vital aspect of a well-rounded life, yet they are distinct paths. Imagine navigating this circle, understanding how each choice intertwines yet stands separate, forming the foundation of a fulfilling life. This analogy can help you reflect on how to balance these spheres, especially after achieving financial freedom.

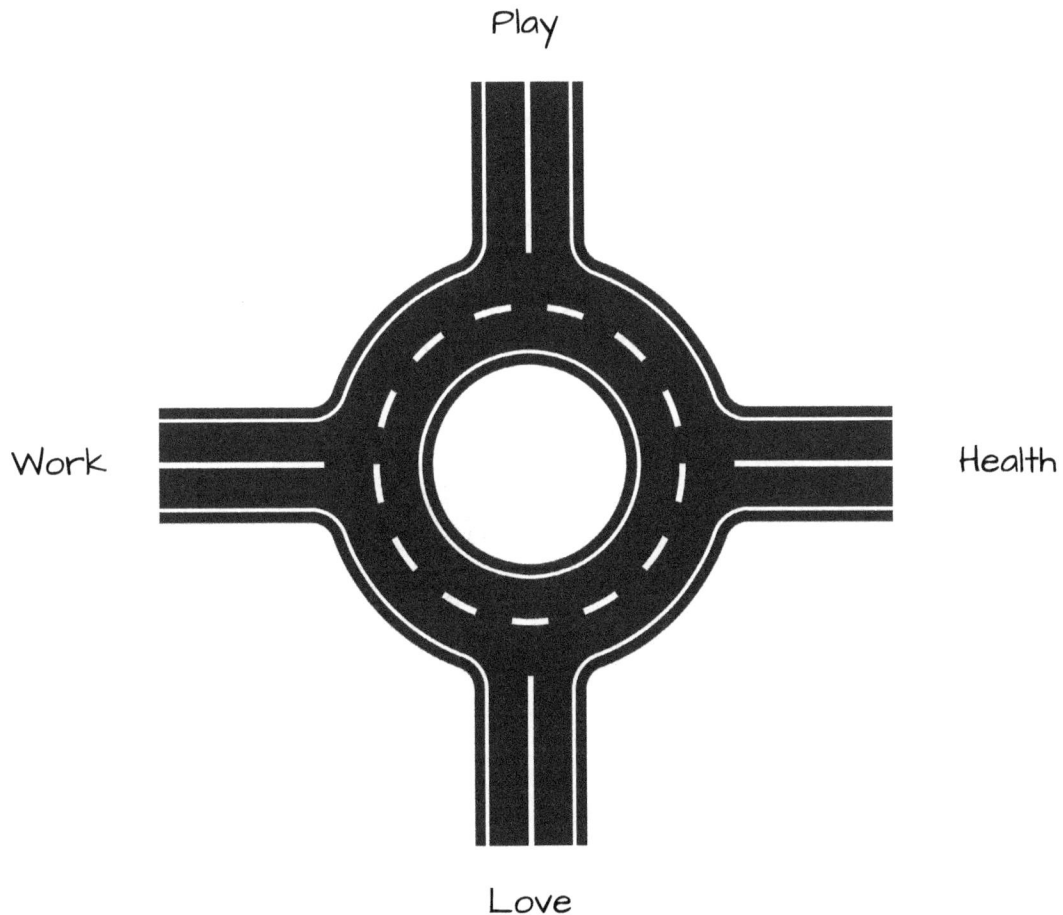

The World of Work

You've hit the milestone of financial freedom. Now, do you ease off the gas, switch routes, or keep speeding towards even greater financial heights? As you ponder this crossroads, let's delve into key considerations that can help guide your decision. Reflect on what financial freedom truly means to you and how it aligns with your life goals. Is it about more leisure time, new ventures, or perhaps a mix of both? Analyzing these aspects will help you steer your journey in a direction that not only maintains your financial stability but also enriches your life beyond the numbers.

In the journey beyond financial freedom, your work approach can vary greatly. Here are four styles.

- **Full-Steam Ahead** - you maintain a full-time career or dive into an all-consuming entrepreneurial venture.
- **Moderated Pace** - you might shift to part-time work or a role that's less demanding, balancing your professional and personal life.
- **Occasional Engagement** - you prefer sporadic work like consulting or freelancing, where flexibility and personal interest take precedence.
- **Sabbatical** - you step away from formal work entirely for a while, giving you time to indulge in hobbies, travel, or volunteer work, keeping the door open to return to professional life later.

Shade in the circle next to the work style that resonates most with you. Underneath, jot down your thoughts or feelings about why this particular form of work appeals to you. Reflect on how it aligns with your current lifestyle, personal goals, and the type of balance you want to maintain post-financial freedom.

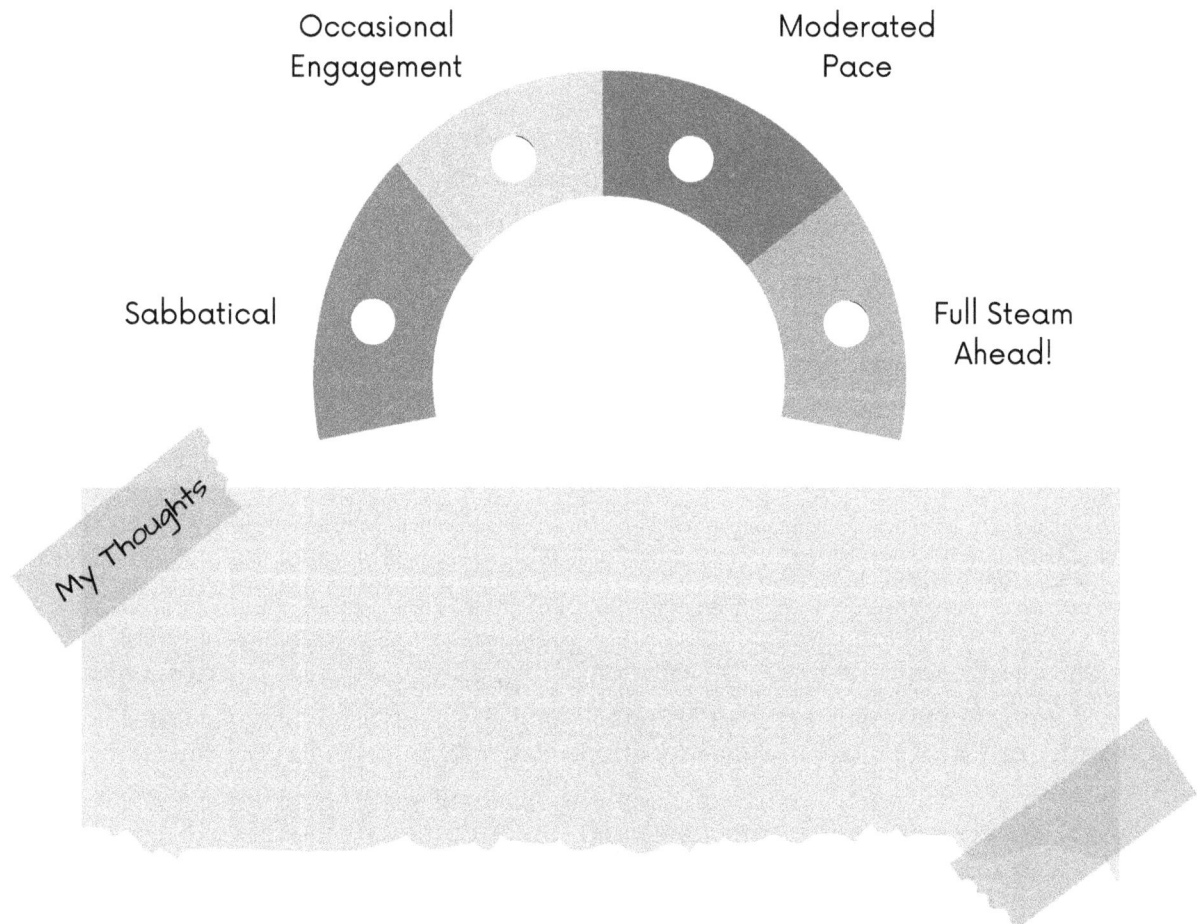

Occasional Engagement

Moderated Pace

Sabbatical

Full Steam Ahead!

My Thoughts

Play More!

Here's the best part of financial freedom - you can play more! Let's look at four levels of play.

- **Active Exploration** - you dive into a variety of activities, like extensive traveling, discovering new hobbies, or mastering new skills.
- **Regular Leisure** - you consistently participate in your favorite leisure activities, whether it's a weekly sports match, joining book clubs, or attending regular art or music classes.
- **Casual Enjoyment** - you engage in hobbies and trips occasionally, fitting them into your schedule as it suits you.
- **Relaxed Downtime** - you focus on more tranquil pursuits like reading, gardening, or simply enjoying the serenity of nature.

Shade in the circle beside the play style that most aligns with your interests. Below, share your thoughts or feelings on why this particular approach to leisure and enjoyment stands out to you. Reflect on how it fits into your life post-financial freedom and contributes to your overall happiness and well-being.

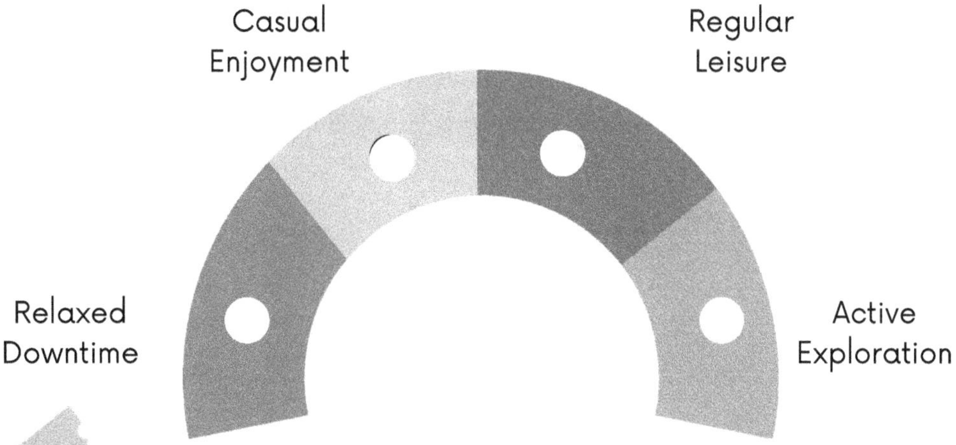

Casual
Enjoyment

Regular
Leisure

Relaxed
Downtime

Active
Exploration

My Thoughts

Mind your Health

Health encompasses physical, mental, and emotional well-being.

- **Integrated Well-Being** - you create a holistic integration of health into daily life, characterized by regular exercise, balanced nutrition, and emotional wellness.
- **Balanced Health Focus** - you maintain a steady, balanced approach to health without letting it overshadow other life areas, including moderate exercise and mindful eating.
- **General Health Consciousness** - you have a flexible awareness of health, encompassing occasional fitness activities and general healthy eating habits.
- **Casual Health Attention** - you adopt a laid-back approach, with minimal active pursuit of health routines, focusing on convenience and immediate preferences rather than structured health management.

Shade in the circle next to the health style that aligns with your vision of a financially free lifestyle. Then share your thoughts about the approach you selected.

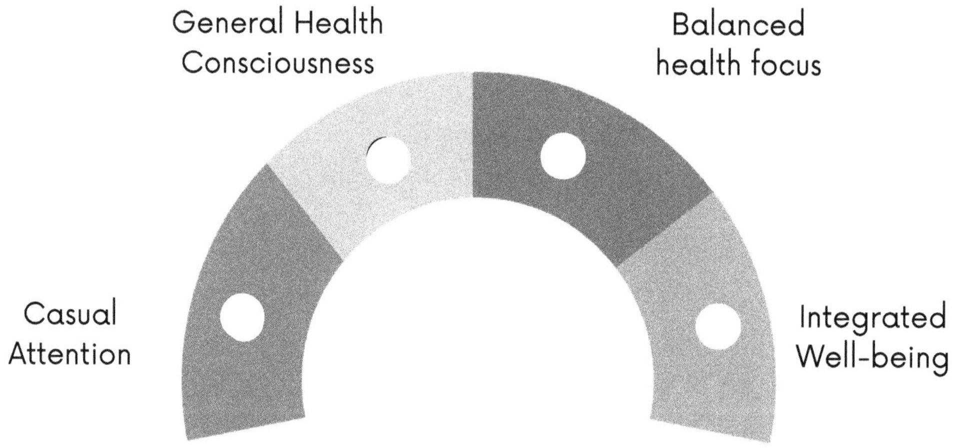

General Health
Consciousness

Balanced
health focus

Casual
Attention

Integrated
Well-being

My Thoughts

Keep your Heart open to Love

The term 'love' encompasses relationships, connections, and community involvement.

- **Deeply Connected** - you actively nurture and deepen relationships, be it with family, friends, or within the community.
- **Balanced Engagement** - you regularly interact and connect with loved ones and the community, ensuring a harmonious balance between social activities and personal time.
- **Casual Connectivity** - you engage in social activities and relationships as part of an overall lifestyle equilibrium.
- **Selective Interaction** - you take a more reserved approach, focusing on a few key relationships or social engagements, with a greater emphasis on personal space and selective social involvement.

Shade in the circle beside the 'love' tier that resonates with your vision of a financially free lifestyle. Then, in the space below, describe why this particular approach to relationships and social engagement appeals to you.

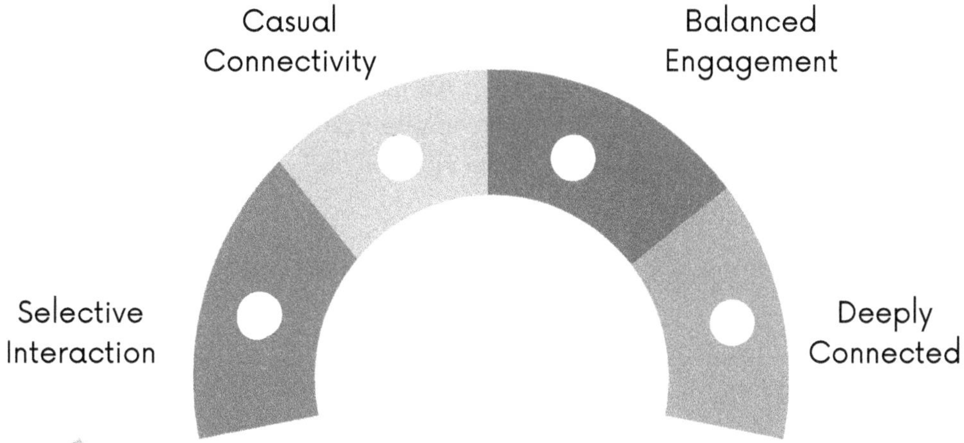

Casual
Connectivity

Balanced
Engagement

Selective
Interaction

Deeply
Connected

My Thoughts

This activity highlights a crucial insight: aside from the work sphere, achieving the ideal levels in love, play, and health doesn't hinge on financial freedom. You have the power to shape these areas of your life according to your desires, regardless of your financial status. Answer the questions below to create a roadmap to a more balanced and fulfilling life in all aspects, not just financially.

> **"Happiness is not something ready-made. It comes from your own actions."**
> **- Dalai Lama**

WORK

What's your ideal **work** scenario now that you're financially free?

Identify one or two changes that can move you closer to this scenario.

PLAY

What leisure activities do you value most?

Think of a small step you can take to incorporate more of these activities into your routine.

LOVE

Which relationships are most important to you?

Consider one action you can take to strengthen these connections.

What does being healthy look like for you?

Identify one habit you can start or improve to enhance your health.

A New Horizon: Jenna and Elise's Journey to Harmonious Living

Jenna and Elise's story unfolds like a carefully crafted tapestry, woven with dreams, love, and the pursuit of a life less ordinary. Both in their early forties, they had reached a point where financial freedom wasn't just a distant dream but a tangible reality. As they embarked on this new chapter, they set about to design their lives, examining the spheres of work, love, play, and health.

Jenna, once a high-flying lawyer, and Elise, a Benefits Specialist, had thrived in their careers. Yet, beneath the surface, a longing for change simmered. Embracing their newfound freedom, Jenna shifted to "Moderated Pace," working a limited schedule for non-profit organizations. Meanwhile, Elise opted for a one-year "Sabbatical," to write and design a graphic novel and explore jewelry design. She transformed her her work into a source of joy rather than just obligation.

Their home, a cozy bungalow adorned with Elise's art and Jenna's collection of vintage books, became a nurturing haven for their relationship. Prioritizing "Deeply Connected" interactions, they dedicated time to nurturing their bond, be it through quiet evenings under the starry sky in their backyard or through shared laughter over homemade meals. Their love for each other blossomed, grounded in mutual respect and the joy of shared experiences. Community engagement, especially within the local LGBTQ+ scene, enriched their lives with diverse, meaningful connections.

Adventure beckoned them with an irresistible allure. Their shared passion for travel evolved into "Active Exploration." They wandered through the streets of Paris, soaked up the sun in the Greek Isles, and hiked through the majestic trails of the Canadian Rockies. Back home, Elise rekindled her love for pottery, while Jenna found solace in gardening, their hobbies offering both relaxation and a sense of accomplishment.

Together, they embarked on a journey of "Balanced Health Focus." Mornings started with yoga in their sunlit living room, followed by nutritious, thoughtfully prepared breakfasts. They embraced mental and emotional well-being through meditation and by joining a local mindfulness group, finding peace in the tranquility of self-reflection and shared spiritual journeys.

In this tapestry of their new life, Jenna and Elise discovered a deeper connection, not just with each other, but with their inner selves. Their story is a mosaic of moments— some monumental, some fleeting—all adding up to a life rich in love, purpose, and joy.

Don't wait for opportunity, create it

Practice Resilience

You've successfully navigated the challenging journey to financial freedom, overcoming roadblocks and weathering storms along the way. Now, as you cruise towards financial independence, you're equipped with confidence, knowledge, and the experience of triumphs and trials. Embrace this chance to redefine the ordinary and make bold, life-affirming choices.

Yet, life's constant is change. Each new day ushers in fresh opportunities and potential shifts in circumstances. What we have today may evolve or fade tomorrow, serving as a poignant reminder to savor the present. Fortunately, you're armed with the right tools to adapt to any curveball life throws your way. Let's delve into how you can effectively navigate four potential events: recessions, global events, job loss, and health crises.

Recessions

Navigating through economic downturns and recessions is like driving through unexpected fog on your road trip to financial freedom. Sure, seeing your investment dashboard flash with big drops might give you that roller-coaster stomach drop, but remember, it's more like a paper detour than a real crash. The key? Don't hit the panic button and sell your investments. Instead, think of a recession as a pop-up sale, offering unique opportunities to pick up valuable assets at a discount.

Now, if you find yourself tracking every twist and turn of the market, it might be time to ease off the gas pedal. It's a signal to check in with your risk tolerance. Are you the type to cruise comfortably with a bit more stashed in your savings tank, or are you thrilled by the prospect of scooping up undervalued stocks that can turbocharge your long-term goals? Recessions, much like sharp bends on a scenic route, test your financial driving skills and strategy. They're a chance to reassess your route, ensuring it aligns with your adventure spirit and destination dreams.

> **"Resilience is knowing that you are the only one that has the power and the responsibility to pick yourself up."**
> **- Mary Holloway**

Global Events

Buckle up, because in this global village, what happens on one side of the world can send ripples all the way to your doorstep. Wars and global pandemics, for instance, can jolt our financial, mental, and emotional well-being. Just think about the pandemic's impact: once-bustling streets turning eerily silent, favorite shops boarding up, jobs disappearing like morning mist. It's akin to navigating through a dense, unpredictable fog. Yet, in these challenging times, the most creative minds find new paths. They pivot to the digital highway, innovate with delivery services, and even add flair to safety with funky, personalized masks. Such times remind us that our journey's beauty lies beyond material wealth. They underscore the importance of health, community, and bouncing back with resilience.

Now, let's talk about another ongoing event—climate change. Imagine it as a long, uphill climb on your journey. It's not just about hotter summers or colder winters; it's about shifting weather patterns that can affect everything from food prices to insurance costs. But, as savvy travelers on this road, we can take steps to adapt and even help mitigate its impacts. Maybe it's investing in companies committed to sustainability, or perhaps it's tweaking our daily habits to be more eco-friendly, like choosing an electric vehicle for our road trip. Climate change is our call to action, urging us not just to be passengers on this planet, but responsible stewards. Our choices on this journey can paint a future that's not only vibrant for us but also nurturing for our planet.

Job Loss

Cruising down your career highway with the wind in your hair, everything seems perfect – until it's not. Out of the blue, your career road takes a sharp turn: the company changes hands, the economic landscape shifts causing layoffs, or maybe the new boss's style is cramping your groove. Even the most passionate professionals can hit burnout when the workplace vibe turns sour. Remember, these bumps in the road are exactly why you embarked on the journey to financial freedom!

But here's an adventurous twist: sometimes, losing your job is like finding an unexpected shortcut to your dreams. It can be the nudge you need to re-route towards a lifestyle that's more you, to discover work that really lights your fire, or hey, to simply park by the beach and enjoy some well-deserved downtime. Think of it as an unplanned pit stop that gives you a chance to refuel, reassess, and rev up for the next exciting leg of your journey. It's all part of the grand adventure of life, where sometimes the detours turn out to be the most scenic routes!

Health Crisis

Riding down the highway of life, we often cruise at full speed, not thinking much about our physical, mental, and emotional health. But sometimes, life throws a wrench into the gears: a health crisis. Suddenly, we're veering off course, navigating through a maze of insurance claims, sky-high medical bills, and financial stresses that make the journey bumpier.

If you've built a high-octane work pace, it could be fueling some of your health problems. This might be the perfect moment to tap the brakes and reevaluate. Financial freedom is your trusty GPS, guiding you to a destination that resonates with your heart and soul. But what good is reaching that dream destination if your health, the engine driving you, is sputtering? Health crises can redirect your path in ways you never expected.

Build an Action Plan

Gear up for a smoother ride on your financial road trip by prepping for unexpected detours ahead of time. Being prepared not only gives you a sense of control but also lights up the path forward. Let's get you ready for any bumps on the road.

Mark an 'X' in the circle next to the event you're gearing up for. If you have a different scenario in mind, no worries! Just write it in.

◯ Recession   ◯ Global Event   ◯ Job Loss   ◯ Health Crisis

◯ Other _____

Write a brief description of the chosen event and how it could potentially impact your life. Consider financial, emotional, and lifestyle aspects.

Map out three smart moves you can make right now to stay ahead of the game. For example, if you selected health crisis, take steps to improve your nutrition and fitness level; for a job loss, how about updating your resume and networking.

1.

2.

3.

Jot down some things you can do in the immediate aftermath of the event. For example, in the case of a recession, list out potential cost-cutting measures or investment strategies.

Fantastic work! You've now equipped yourself with the ultimate toolkit to handle life's unexpected turns. Remember, you're resilient, strong, and absolutely unstoppable. With these plans in place, you're more than ready to cruise through any challenges with confidence and grace.

you are
AMAZING

Create a Joy-Filled Life

We've now come to the grand finale of our thrilling Money Road Trip, and there's one vital takeaway I want to leave you with: Seek out joy. Make it the cornerstone of your journey. Envision joy as the radiant sun at the center of your life's galaxy, with all else gracefully orbiting it. But let's be clear: this isn't about the fleeting happiness that comes and goes like a flash in the night sky. I'm talking about a profound, soul-warming joy, the kind that illuminates your path and gently sweeps away worries like dew in the dawn light.

And how will you recognize this joy when it arrives? Oh, believe me, you'll know. Your smile will turn into a beacon of light, and you'll find yourself thinking, "I wish I could capture this moment and keep it forever." A friend once described these instances as "dandelion moments." Picture a dandelion, its head brimming with seeds. With a gentle gust, these seeds dance into the air. Each one represents a dandelion moment – brief, yet filled with unbridled joy and wonder. By acknowledging and savoring these moments, we invite a cascade of them into our lives. Just imagine, looking back over the years and seeing a trail of these dandelion moments, painting a picture of a life rich with joy – isn't that the ultimate dream?

Now, think about shaping your days with these joyous moments in mind. By focusing on the simple pleasures, we can also ease off the financial throttle because, in truth, our needs are often less than we think. Could the key to a life brimming with joy be this straightforward? Embrace this idea, and watch as your world transforms, one dandelion moment at a time.

Dr. Brenda's Dandelion Moments

I vividly recall a September day, under the bright Virginia Beach sun, with my little girl perched high on my shoulders, giggling with delight as a parade unfurled before us. My parents were visiting, and the air was filled with the joy and laughter of a family weekend. As the Shriners zipped past in their quirky little cars, a profound emotion swept over me, bringing unexpected tears to my eyes. This moment held a special magic. Just two months prior, I had first held my daughter in an orphanage halfway across the world in Ukraine. That day, as we watched the parade together, surrounded by the loving presence of her grandparents, I was struck by the realization of our new family bond. It was a poignant, heartwarming snapshot in time – a true dandelion moment.

My dad, a man of few words, found solace in the quiet rhythms of farming life, the predictability of weather talk, and the steady devotion to the Packers. But within the electrifying atmosphere of Lambeau Field, he transformed into someone else – FUN DAD. I vividly recall a crisp autumn day, just him and me, nestled among a sea of green and gold fans on the stadium's bleachers. The game was in full swing, the air crackling with excitement. Then, in a moment of athletic brilliance, the wide receive catches a long pass, gracefully charging into the end zone. TOUCHDOWN! In an instant, the crowd erupted. Dad and I were on our feet, caught up in the wave of euphoria, our voices merging with the roar of tens of thousands. We clapped, cheered, and exchanged triumphant high-fives, our spirits soaring with the team's success. In that moment, the usual barriers of daily life dissolved. There was just the joy of the game, the bond between father and child, and the shared thrill of victory.

Nestled in the heart of Zion National Park, I struck gold with a picturesque RV spot in Watchman Campground. Surrounded by nature's splendor, the day unwinds with a scenic hike, leading me back to my cozy campsite by the soothing sounds of the Virgin River. There, in the warmth of a campfire, with the tranquil music of the river playing in the background, I watch in awe as the sky transitions into a canvas of stars, each one twinkling like a promise of endless possibilities. The campfire crackles, sending sparks dancing into the night air, and I feel an overwhelming sense of connection to the world around me. In this moment, my soul is aglow, fully immersed in the beauty and serenity of nature.

> **"I'm somewhere beautiful in the world, looking out over a vista, totally relaxed knowing there are friends somewhere close at hand and my son living his best life."**
> **- Susan R.**

Instead of a flyover trip, we spent a day visiting the small towns of Ecuador, eating homemade ice cream and trying fruits we had never seen before. My 10 year old son at my side, when not entertaining all the other tourists on the bus. The culture, the people, the beauty of that trip, shared with my favorite person who fits in everywhere. That was a dandelion moment for me. - Susan R.

Enjoying an amazing Italian 4-course meal with the wine flowing, shared with a community of new friends from the UK. We were a collection of single parents with our kids, on a working farm, where we learned how to make traditional Italian dishes with ingredients we had collected from the farm earlier in the day. . . . A week in the mountains north of Venice, in the fresh air, sunshine, and farm life, we turned into best friends that have stayed in touch for years, watching each others children grow up and become young adults. - Susan R.

> **"I can still feel the freedom as my feet left the pavement, hands held tightly in trust as I swung back and forth, with a big smile on my face."**
> **- Janine M.**

I was a little girl, being swung down the street by my Aunt and cousin. They were fun. Much more fun than my own family. They were visiting and took me out for a walk. I was probably around 8 years old, . . . I felt a big sense of fun and freedom, and most importantly, that I was loved. I didn't feel that at home, so when they took me for a walk and played with me, just me . . . I felt significant. . . . I can still feel the freedom as my feet left the pavement, hands held tightly in trust as I swung back and forth, with a big smile on my face. Fun. Freedom. Trust. Significance. Safety. It's one of my first memories where I felt these feelings. - Janine M.

My Dandelion Moments

AWESOME!

You made it! Hats off to you for reaching the exhilarating milestone of financial freedom. This is more than just a finish line – it's a golden opportunity to pause, reflect, and sculpt the life you've always imagined. Now's the time to mold your destination into whatever shape brings you the most joy. Let's take a quick look back at the key takeaways from this chapter, each a stepping stone to crafting your ideal future.

☐ You designed your life.

You've skillfully used engineering principles to design a lifestyle that reflects your values and aspirations. With a clear vision, you're shaping your life's spheres - work, play, love, and health - to align with your personal ideals. Crucially, you're already making strides, setting the foundation for a future that resonates with your idea of perfect balance.

☐ You created an action plan for events that may interrupt your journey.

You've turbocharged your resilience by proactively thinking about potential obstacles that could throw a wrench in your journey. Whether it's a recession, global crisis, job loss, or health issue, you're not just prepared, you're strategically equipped. With a well-thought-out response plan, you stand ready and unshakable. You're not just prepared; you embody resilience and strength.

☐ You are dedicated to creating a joy-filled life.

Life is a collection of moments, each one precious and unique. As you start to identify those 'dandelion moments' – those magical instances when everything aligns perfectly and joy overflows – you'll learn to create even more of them. By centering your life around these bursts of joy, you'll craft a journey so fulfilling that looking back won't even cross your mind.

Notes

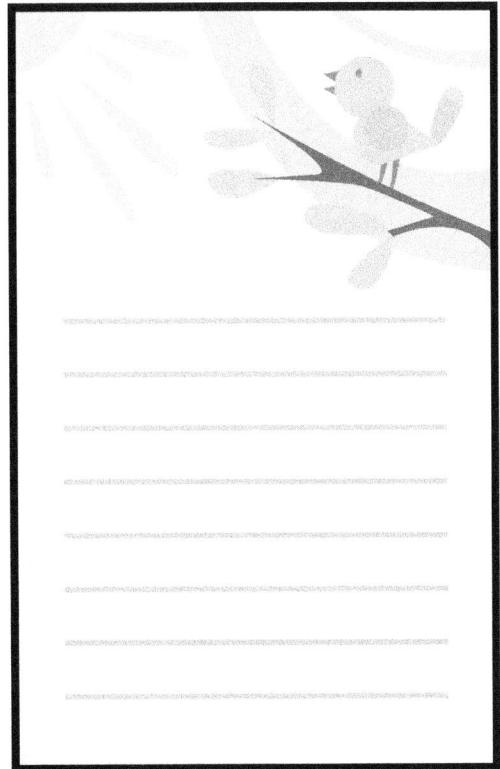

BONUS

GOAL GETTING WORKSHEETS

Get your Goals!

Setting goals is fantastic, but achieving them? That's where the real magic happens. Dive into these worksheets to chart out your goals and track your progress for the upcoming year and months. Embrace the journey of turning aspirations into achievements. And don't forget to shape your goals to be SMARTER – specific, measurable, attainable, relevant, time-bound, evaluate, and reward. Let's turn those dreams into reality!

SMARTER =
- Specific
- Measurable
- Actionable
- Relevant
- Time-bound
- Evaluate
- Reward

GOAL GETTING PLAN

YEAR:

GOAL

PURPOSE

MOTIVATION

START DATE

END DATE

REWARD

OBSTACLES TO OVERCOME

RESOURCES

BIG STEPS

LITTLE STEPS

NOTES

GOAL GETTING PLAN

GOAL

PURPOSE

MOTIVATION

START DATE

END DATE

REWARD

OBSTACLES TO OVERCOME

RESOURCES

BIG STEPS

LITTLE STEPS

NOTES

GOAL GETTING PLAN

GOAL

PURPOSE

MOTIVATION

START DATE

END DATE

REWARD

OBSTACLES TO OVERCOME

RESOURCES

BIG STEPS

LITTLE STEPS

NOTES

GOAL GETTING PLAN

GOAL

PURPOSE

MOTIVATION

START DATE

END DATE

REWARD

OBSTACLES TO OVERCOME

RESOURCES

BIG STEPS

LITTLE STEPS

NOTES

GOAL GETTING PLAN

APRIL

| GOAL | PURPOSE | MOTIVATION |

| START DATE | END DATE | REWARD |

| OBSTACLES TO OVERCOME | RESOURCES |

| BIG STEPS | LITTLE STEPS | NOTES |

GOAL GETTING PLAN

MAY

GOAL

PURPOSE

MOTIVATION

START DATE

END DATE

REWARD

OBSTACLES TO OVERCOME

RESOURCES

BIG STEPS

LITTLE STEPS

NOTES

GOAL GETTING PLAN

GOAL

PURPOSE

MOTIVATION

START DATE

END DATE

REWARD

OBSTACLES TO OVERCOME

RESOURCES

BIG STEPS

LITTLE STEPS

NOTES

GOAL GETTING PLAN

GOAL

PURPOSE

MOTIVATION

START DATE

END DATE

REWARD

OBSTACLES TO OVERCOME

RESOURCES

BIG STEPS

LITTLE STEPS

NOTES

GOAL GETTING PLAN

GOAL

PURPOSE

MOTIVATION

START DATE

END DATE

REWARD

OBSTACLES TO OVERCOME

RESOURCES

BIG STEPS

LITTLE STEPS

NOTES

GOAL GETTING PLAN

GOAL

PURPOSE

MOTIVATION

START DATE

END DATE

REWARD

OBSTACLES TO OVERCOME

RESOURCES

BIG STEPS

LITTLE STEPS

NOTES

GOAL GETTING PLAN

OCTOBER

GOAL

PURPOSE

MOTIVATION

START DATE

END DATE

REWARD

OBSTACLES TO OVERCOME

RESOURCES

BIG STEPS

LITTLE STEPS

NOTES

GOAL GETTING PLAN

GOAL

PURPOSE

MOTIVATION

START DATE

END DATE

REWARD

OBSTACLES TO OVERCOME

RESOURCES

BIG STEPS

LITTLE STEPS

NOTES

GOAL GETTING PLAN

GOAL

PURPOSE

MOTIVATION

START DATE

END DATE

REWARD

OBSTACLES TO OVERCOME

RESOURCES

BIG STEPS

LITTLE STEPS

NOTES

www.ingramcontent.com/pod-product-compliance
Lightning Source LLC
Chambersburg PA
CBHW051752200326
41597CB00025B/4534